HIGH-LIGHTS
OF THE
BIBLE

William L. Lane

Regal Books

A Division of G/L Publications
Ventura, CA, U.S.A.

Other good reading in
Bible Commentary for Laymen Series:
Highlights of the Bible–Genesis to Nehemiah
by Ray C. Stedman
How It all Began–Genesis 1–11
by Ronald Youngblood
Letters to Children of Light–1,2,3 John
by E.M. Blaiklock
Highlights of the Bible–Poets and Prophets
by Ray C. Stedman

The foreign language publishing of all Regal Books is under the direction of GLINT. GLINT provides financial and technical help for the adaptation, translation and publishing of books in more than 85 languages for millions of people worldwide.

For more information write: GLINT, P.O. Box 6688, Ventura, California 93006.

Scripture quotations in this publication, unless otherwise indicated, are from the *(NIV)* the *New International Version*, Holy Bible. Copyright © 1978 by New York International Bible Society. Used by permission. Other versions quoted are:
RSV–Revised Standard Version of the Bible, copyrighted 1946 and 1952 by the Division of Christian Education of the NCCC, U.S.A., and used by permission.
NEB–From the New English Bible. © The Delegates of the Oxford University Press and the Syndics of the Cambridge University Press 1961, 1970. Reprinted by permission.

Second Printing, 1981

Published by Regal Books
A Division of GL Publications
Ventura, California 93006
Printed in U.S.A.

Library of Congress Catalog Card No. 80-50543
ISBN 0-8307-0676-3

CONTENTS

Author's Preface   5

1. A Pamphlet for Hard Times   7
The Gospel of Mark

2. Blessings for the Nations   16
The Gospel of Matthew

3. A Defense of the Faith   25
Luke–Acts

4. A Witness to the Truth   35
The Gospel of John

5. Mission and Church Nurture   45
First and Second Thessalonians

6. Confusion and Crisis   55
First and Second Corinthians

7. The Truth of the Gospel   65
Galatians

8. Commitment to Mission   73
Romans

9. Mandate for Maturity   81
Colossians; Philemon; Ephesians

10. Partners in Mission   *89*
    Philippians

11. Church Order   *99*
    Titus; First and Second Timothy

12. Encouragement and Warning   *107*
    Hebrews

13. Practical Righteousness   *117*
    James

14. Assault Upon the Church   *127*
    First and Second Peter; Jude

15. The Tests of Christian Life and Fellowship   *137*
    First, Second, and Third John

16. The Triumph of God   *147*
    Revelation

Notes   *157*

A Gospel Light Teacher's Manual and Student
Discovery Guide for Bible study groups using
Highlights of the Bible: New Testament are available
from your church supplier.

AUTHOR'S PREFACE

The invitation to prepare a brief introduction to the books of the New Testament in the series, "Highlights of the Bible," was welcome. My courses at a state university have provided me with a workshop for exploring these documents of the church with several generations of students. I have discovered that when a New Testament book is placed in the setting of a particular community, the writer's statement becomes meaningful as a response to specific questions and problems. The fact that he wrote to instruct, comfort, challenge or rebuke actual persons can be appreciated. In every instance writing is a substitute for the personal presence of a church leader who was responding to the needs of the churches.

It is this approach I have followed in preparing this book. I have tried to sketch the life situation that accounts for the writing of a Gospel, a letter or a sermon, and to show how distinctive emphases within each of the New Testament documents are a pastoral response to that situation.

The consideration of the Gospels begins with Mark because I am persuaded that Mark is the earliest Gospel. Luke and Acts are presented together not simply because they have a common authorship but because they are two volumes of a single work. The treatment of the letters of Paul seeks to arrange them in the order of their appearance, beginning with the two letters to the Christians in Thessalonica. In the remaining books of the New Testament I have followed the order of the canon, with the single exception of grouping Jude with the letters of Peter.

I wish to acknowledge the strong support of my wife Brenda, who helped me to remember that I am writing for lay men and women, and who typed the manuscript of this book.

William L. Lane

William L. Lane
Western Kentucky University
Bowling Green, Kentucky

A PAMPHLET FOR
HARD TIMES
The Gospel of Mark

Trial by Fire

A.D. 64 is remembered as the year of the great fire in Rome. For the Christian community, gathering in house-churches throughout the city, this year had begun like any other year.

Although the Christians were sometimes a topic for pagan gossip, the popular misrepresentations had not affected the growth of the movement. It was said that Christians were atheists because they refused to represent their God by an image. It was whispered that they were cannibals because they spoke of eating the flesh and drinking the blood of their Lord. They were taunted as incestuous because they called one another "Brother" and "Sister," and held their most sacred rites in connection with a meal they called the *Agape*, or love-feast, at which only Christians were permitted to be present. They were scorned as those who hated other men because they refused to attend the spectacles in the circus or arena and kept themselves from the temples and pleasure arcades of the city. But there had been no police action against the Christians.

All of that changed in the aftermath of a devastating fire which threatened to reduce the Eternal City to ash and rubble. The fire broke out in the congested area around the Great Circus, with its cluttered shops and sprawling slum. Then a shift in the wind carried the violent flames to the adjacent Palatine Hill district, the site of the oldest settlement in Rome where Senators had built their homes among the venerable monuments of past Roman conquests. From there it spread rapidly throughout the city. When after six days it was thought the fire was under control, it broke out again and raged unchecked for two more weeks. Of the 14 districts of the city, only four were untouched by the flames. Three were leveled to the ground.

Nero had been absent from the city and returned only when his own palace was threatened. He responded to the disaster by ordering the construction of emergency accommodations for the homeless and the distribution of food brought in from neighboring towns. In the subsequent months he entered into an elaborate program of urban renewal, clearing debris and erecting houses, parks and streets at government expense. But these measures failed to win him any popular support. The people were seething with resentment. They firmly believed that the emperor himself had ordered the fire. He had done so because he intended to construct a new palace in the vicinity of the Great Circus. This suspicion was fueled by the persistent rumor that while the city was burning Nero had gone upon his private stage and celebrated the calamity by singing about the destruction by fire of ancient Troy.

It was to distract attention from such rumors that Nero ordered the imperial police to act against the Christians. "To suppress this rumor," the Roman historian Tacitus writes, "Nero fabricated scapegoats, and punished with every refinement the notoriously depraved Christians (as they were popularly called.)" Recognized Christians were arrested and tortured. On the basis of their information large numbers of others were herded before Roman magistrates and condemned to death—not for the crime of arson, but because popular prejudice permitted the humiliation of the Christians. Tacitus writes: "Their deaths were made farcical. Dressed in wild animals' skins, they were torn to pieces by dogs, or crucified, or made into torches to be ignited after dark as a substitute for daylight. Nero provided his Gardens for the spectacle, and exhibited displays in the Circus, at which he mingled with the crowd, or stood in a chariot, dressed as a charioteer."

But he adds, "Despite their guilt as Christians, and the ruthless punishment it deserved, the victims were pitied. For it was felt that they were being sacrificed to one man's brutality rather than to the national interest."[1]

That turn of events forced the Christian community to go underground, literally. The catacombs, with their series of narrow underground tunnels and tomb-chambers cut in the soft rock, were regarded as places of sanctuary that might be exempt from police intrusion. In the climate of uncertainty created by the emperor's action, Christians fled to the catacombs. Christian commitment could result in a martyr's death.

A Pastoral Response

Among the Christian leaders in Rome was John Mark of Jerusalem. His presence in the city when the persecution began is certain from the closing greeting in Peter's letter of warning to the churches of Asia Minor. Describing Rome by the code word "Babylon" (where Christians were now exiled and captive, even as Israel had been earlier), Peter conveys the greetings of the church and of "my son Mark" (1 Pet. 5:13). The context speaks ominously of "suffering as a Christian" at a time when vindication can be expected only from God (1 Pet. 4:12-19).

Like the apostle Peter, Mark recognized that frightened men and women would need to be strengthened before the testing of their faith. He prepared the earliest of the Gospels as a pastoral response to the crisis at Rome. His work can be described as a pamphlet for hard times. It is directed to a church which was the object of imperial persecution following the great fire. In the simple language of the marketplace, Mark brought together an account of Jesus' deeds and words which addressed the Christians of Rome with the directness characteristic of an apostolic sermon. The witness borne to Jesus was a remarkable record of Jesus' commitment to His own followers, even when they failed to understand the significance of rejection, suffering and death in God's plan for Him, and for them.

When it is remembered that Mark wrote to strengthen Christians and to provide them with a basis for faithfulness to Jesus at a time when Christian life was defined by the catacombs or the arena, the details of the Gospel take on added significance. The evangelist shows that a Christian can suffer no form of humiliation that has not been endured already by Jesus, his Lord.

Only Mark records that in the wilderness Jesus was "with the wild beasts" (Mark 1:13, *RSV*). That detail was filled with meaning for Christians exposed to the arena where they might stand helpless in the presence of wild beasts. Were Christians misrepresented and falsely labeled by pagans in Rome? Jesus had been labeled as deranged by His family (3:21) and as demonic by officials from Jerusalem (3:22-30). Were Christians sometimes betrayed to the authorities from within the circle of intimate friends? One of Jesus' own disciples was Judas Iscariot, "who betrayed him" (3:19). In the Gospel prepared by Mark, Christians discovered that nothing which they might suffer at the hands of the government had been alien to the experience of Jesus.

Moreover, Jesus had spoken openly of the persecution that could be expected in the Christian life. He had warned about those who "have no root in themselves, but endure for a while; then, when tribulation or persecution arises on account of the word, immediately they fall away" (4:17, *RSV*). Mark recalled a sobering word of Jesus that no other evangelist chose to record: "Everyone will be salted with fire" (9:49). When Jesus had promised those who followed Him "houses and brothers and sisters and mothers and children and lands," He had added significantly, "with persecutions" (10:30, *RSV*). Jesus warned that the day would come when those who were identified with Him would be beaten and would stand before governors and kings for His sake as witnesses to the truth. He had not kept from His disciples the cruel truth that brother would betray brother to death, and the father his child, and children their parents, and that His followers would be hated by all men because they belong to Him (13:9-13). In the key statement on discipleship, Jesus had demanded a radical surrender of life and cross-bearing in response to His call (8:34-38). That was now an actual experience for Mark's readers in Rome. It had been the experience of Jesus as well, preceded by a trial before a Roman magistrate, scourging with the dreaded bone-tipped flagellum, and the cruel mockery of the local soldiers (15:15-20).

It was the threat of such treatment that might motivate a person to deny that Jesus was his Lord. But if he did so, he would save his life only to experience rejection when Jesus returned at the last day in triumphal procession with the holy angels (8:35-38). Mark remembered, with obvious satisfaction, that it was a Roman who, when he saw the manner in which Jesus died, exclaimed, "Surely this man was the Son of God!" (15:39).

The details of Mark's Gospel are charged with meaning for men and women who were treated with contempt and humiliated because they bore the name of Jesus. Jesus had not rejected suffering and death. They could not do so either. God's approval of the faithful obedience of His Son was evident to everyone when on the third day the tomb in which the crucified body of Jesus had been laid was empty. The final impression left with Mark's reader is the eloquent witness of the empty tomb as interpreted by God's messenger: "Do not be amazed; you seek Jesus of Nazareth, who was crucified. He has risen, he is not here; see the place where they laid him. But go, tell his disciples and Peter that he is going before you to Galilee; there you will see him, as he told you" (16:6,7, *RSV*).

Jesus' resurrection made clear that suffering, humiliation, and death were not the final word on the life of one who trusted God and remained true to Him. The solemn pledge that Jesus would meet with His shattered disciples in Galilee provided the hunted Christians of Rome with the assurance that Jesus remained committed to them as well. The special reference to Peter signified that Jesus' commitment extended even to one who had denied his Lord (14:66-72). Here was a basis for forgiveness for those who had denied they were Christians, and for their persecutors also.

In the pages of the pamphlet prepared by Mark, Christian men and women found encouragement to stand firm in their faith in spite of imperial persecution. The final word did not rest with a Roman magistrate or a brutal emperor. It rests with God who raises the dead, and who displays His glory before an unbelieving world through a people who remain faithful to Him.

The Structure of Confession

Men and women who openly admitted that they were Christians when dragged before a Roman magistrate were known as "confessors." Confessing that "Jesus is Lord," they could not acknowledge the lordship of the Caesar. They were prepared to seal their confession with their lifeblood. This readiness to die for Jesus gave to the term "confessor" (or "martyr") a new meaning. The term originally meant one who bore witness to what he had seen or heard, but now it came to mean one who went to his death for what he believed.

When Mark wrote the opening line of his pamphlet he declared he was prepared to take his place among the ranks of the confessors: "The beginning of the good news concerning Jesus the Messiah, the Son of God" (1:1). Here Mark brings together two old Christian confessions: "Jesus is the Messiah," and, "Jesus is the Son of God." The confession that Jesus is the Messiah affirmed that He was the one anointed by God to redeem the people from their sins. The confession that Jesus is God's Son affirmed that He was the one uniquely qualified to achieve redemption for God's people. Mark stands with the confessors in acknowledging Jesus' dignity as Messiah and Son of God.

The opening verse of the Gospel, however, does more than record the evangelist's own confession. It provides an important clue to the structure of his Gospel. Mark gave to his work the structure of confession. The Gospel falls into two equal halves, and each part finds its climax in one of these two confessions.

The first half of the Gospel extends from 1:1—8:30. Its climax is reached in 8:29 when Peter, a Jew and a representative of the new Israel, openly confesses that Jesus is the Messiah. Every incident recorded in the initial half of Mark's pamphlet has prepared his audience for this moment of recognition and confession. Prior to 8:29, the disciples have responded to Jesus' call (see 1:16-20; 2:13,14; 3:13-19), but it is clear that they do not understand who Jesus is. They pose the question of His identity, but are unprepared to risk a daring response. When, for example, a sudden squall at sea had threatened their safety, and Jesus had calmed the turbulence with His sovereign word, "Quiet! Be still!" His terrified followers could only ask, "Who is this? Even the wind and the waves obey him!" (4:39,41).

The people had their own opinions. The popular consensus was that Jesus was a prophet. But the people were frankly divided over whether He was a recent prophet, John the Baptist brought back from the dead (6:14-16), or the prophet Elijah who had returned to announce the day of final judgment, or one of the prophets from Israel's remote past (8:27,28). Not until Jesus' own pointed question to the Twelve at Caesarea Philippi did He receive the appropriate response, "You are the Messiah" (8:29, *NEB*). Mark anticipated this moment of confession in 1:1, when he spoke of Jesus the Messiah, and when it arrives, the first half of the Gospel is brought to a rapid close.

The second half of the Gospel, which extends from 8:31—16:8, clarifies what it means to confess that Jesus is the Messiah. As a matter of fact, in this period "Messiah" was a rather slippery term. Although everyone knew it signified "the one anointed by God," there was wide disagreement on the content of the term. The word was a magnet attracting different hopes from different groups in Judaism. The term was like an empty container into which everyone poured his own expectations. The disciples were not different from others; they had their own set of expectations.

But Jesus had come from God to fulfill His mission, and He could not permit His disciples to fill the term "Messiah" with their own dreams. That is why He immediately began to define what God intended "Messiah" to mean. When He spoke of a rejected, suffering individual who would be killed, and after three days rise again, Peter was outraged (8:31,32); his definition of

Messiah and the one given by Jesus were poles apart! By recording this painful incident (8:31-33), Mark makes it clear that Peter had uttered the correct words and had made a splendid confession, but that he had no understanding of what God intended those words to mean.

The second half of Mark's account is controlled by the theme of Jesus' journey to Jerusalem where the prophecy of His rejection, suffering, death, and resurrection is fulfilled. A full third of the Gospel is situated in Jerusalem (chaps. 11—16), where Jesus was brought before the Roman magistrate, Pontius Pilate who sentenced Him to be crucified on Golgotha (15:1-20). But the climax of the record comes when the centurion in charge of the execution squad exclaimed, "Surely this man was the Son of God" (15:39).

Mark had pointed forward to this moment of recognition and confession in 1:1 when he spoke of Jesus as "the Son of God." The fact that it was a Roman who uttered these words was undoubtedly significant to the evangelist and to the persecuted Christians of Rome, for this moment of insight came when the centurion saw the manner in which Jesus met His death. Within the structure of confession which Mark gave to the Gospel the Roman is a representative of the Gentile world. In making the confession of Peter and the confession of the Roman centurion the points of climax in the Gospel, Mark emphasizes that Jew and Gentile will join their voices in acknowledging the dignity of Jesus.

2
Blessings for the Nations
The Gospel of Matthew

Missionary Vision

Although Mark had prepared his Gospel for the Christians in Rome, it could not remain the treasured possession of a single community for long. Copies were made and were delivered to centers far beyond the shores of Italy. Wherever it was received church leaders recognized its worth. It was an authoritative witness to Christ because it was faithful to the preaching and teaching received through the apostles. Although Matthew was one of the original Twelve chosen by Jesus (Matt. 9:9; 10:1-3), he did not hesitate to adopt Mark's form and outline when he felt God calling him to prepare a Gospel of his own.

Matthew's immediate concern was evangelism and the nurture of new churches planted in predominantly Gentile communities. His Gospel was prepared to support the missionary interests and concerns of Antioch. Antioch of Syria was the church center which had assumed primary responsibility for the Gentile mission. It was itself a mission station, established through the vision of Christian refugees from Jerusalem who recognized that God intended the gospel message for Gentiles as well as Jews (Acts 11:19-21).

Under the effective leadership of Barnabas and Saul of Tarsus, the young church had flourished. In fact, it was at Antioch that the believers were first called "Christians" (Acts 11:22-26) in distinction from other religious groups in the city. Unselfish concern for others was characteristic of the church (Acts 11:27-30; 12:24). When the Spirit of God, the Lord of the harvest, called for fresh missionary advance, it was provided by the leadership of the church at Antioch (Acts 13:1-3). Paul and Barnabas, and later Paul and Silas, went forth from Antioch as the commissioned representatives of the church, and after each mission they returned to the church to report what God had been pleased to do among the Gentiles (Acts 14:26-28; 15:30-35; 18:18-23; 21:3,4).

The Jerusalem assembly was convened to consider the question of Gentile participation in the worship and witness of the churches in response to a request from the Christian leadership at Antioch (Acts 15:1-6). The outcome of that church council assured the success of the Gentile mission (Acts 15:12-31). Believers in Antioch were committed to the missionary mandate of the church. Matthew had become heir to this rich legacy of mission ary vision when he was called to provide pastoral leadership in Antioch.

The Promise to Abraham

The Gospel that Matthew composed provided strong support for the Gentile mission. The first indication of Matthew's distinctive purpose is provided in the opening line. When the evangelist identifies Jesus as "the son of David, the son of Abraham" (Matt. 1:1), he is asserting that the messianic promises to David (2 Sam. 7:12-16) and to Abraham (Gen. 12:2,3) receive their fulfillment through Jesus. The promise to David concerned a royal Son who would rule God's people, Israel, forever. But Matthew was particularly interested in the promise that through Abraham and his descendants blessing would come upon all the families or nations of the earth (Gen. 12:2,3; 18:18; see also 15:5-7; 17:4-8). That ancient promise anticipated the Gentile mission through which blessing comes to the nations.

The Abrahamic promise provides an important key to Matthew's presentation of Jesus. At the close of the Gospel he cites the words of the risen Lord: "All authority in heaven and earth has been given to me. Go therefore and make disciples of all nations . . . and lo, I am with you always, to the close of the age" (Matt. 28:18-20, *RSV*). For Matthew this is the climax of the good news. The mandate to disciple the nations indicates that the promise to Abraham begins to find its full accomplishment. Blessing for the nations comes through the missionary outreach of the church. Even the ringing assurance of Christ's sustaining presence calls to mind God's promise to Jacob when He renewed the covenant made earlier with Abraham: "Behold, I am with you and will keep you wherever you go" (Gen. 28:15, *RSV*).

Matthew's emphasis upon blessing for the nations is at first surprising. Earlier in the Gospel he records that Jesus had restricted the mission activity of His own disciples: "These twelve Jesus sent out with the following instructions: 'Do not go among the Gentiles or enter any town of the Samaritans. Go rather to the lost sheep of Israel' " (Matt. 10:5,6).

Matthew even remembered that Jesus had since said, "I was sent only to the lost sheep of Israel" (Matt. 15:24). In these statements there seems to be little awareness of the promise to Abraham. In actual fact, the promise was deferred. Jesus' mission was primarily to His own people, Israel. But the death and resurrection of Jesus made possible the mission to the nations. Matthew represents a Jewish Christianity that was fully committed to the task of evangelizing the Gentiles in order to fulfill the ancient promise to Abraham.

A Manual for Church Leaders

Another key to Matthew's purpose is provided in the concluding phrase of Christ's commission, "teaching them to obey everything I have commanded you" (Matt. 28:20). To the question, *Where has Jesus commanded His people?* Matthew answers, *In the Gospel which I have placed in your hands.* Although Matthew's predecessor, Mark, had shown that Jesus taught the people, his Gospel concentrated on Jesus' deeds rather than His words. Matthew determined to supply a more complete account of Jesus' teaching. He reproduced almost all of Mark's content but he also supplied his readers with a large body of Jesus' words on subjects of vital importance to the church. Matthew's Gospel can be regarded as a teaching manual. It was intended primarily for church leaders who were responsible for the Gentile mission and entrusted with the task of instructing new converts.

The description of Matthew as a manual for church leaders, or as a teaching book for Gentiles, takes account of one of the most characteristic features of this Gospel. Matthew arranges the teaching of Jesus into five blocks or units. The clue to his arrangement is found in a formula which is repeated on five different occasions, with only slight variation in the wording: "When Jesus had finished these sayings" (7:28; see also 11:1; 13:53; 19:1; 26:1). Matthew uses this formula as a division marker in the unfolding story of Jesus. Each time the formula occurs it calls attention to the end of a unit of teaching upon a particular theme:

1. The Sermon on the Mount: Jesus' teaching concerning *Kingdom ethics* (5:1—7:27).
2. The Instruction of the Twelve: Jesus' teaching concerning *Kingdom outreach* (10:1-42).
3. The Parables: Jesus' teaching concerning *Kingdom theology,* or the nature of the Kingdom itself (13:1-52).
4. Instruction on Church Discipline: Jesus' teaching concerning *Kingdom life* (18:1-35).
5. The Conversation on the Mount of Olives: Jesus' teaching concerning the *coming of the Kingdom* (24:1—25:46).

Once this pattern is recognized, Matthew's Gospel can be divided easily into five blocks of teaching material separated by five narrative sections.

Matthew may have remembered that in Deuteronomy the several blocks of Moses' teachings are concluded with the formula, "When Moses had finished speaking all these words . . ." (Deut. 32:45, *RSV*). His arrangement helped others to see Jesus as the new Lawgiver, the one who is greater than Moses, whose words laid the foundation for the new Israel.

Matthew's Gospel provided church leaders with a convenient book of reference. In their ministry to the younger churches they found it necessary to deal with a host of questions. For example, they were asked: How are Christians to relate to one another? How is a Christian to respond when he encounters hostility from a pagan world? What about the brother who sins? How important is the Jewish law? Why do people reject the witness of the church? When will the Kingdom that Jesus proclaimed come? Had God turned His back upon the Jews? Does the coming of God's Kingdom depend upon the completion of the missionary task?

When they met questions such as these, church leaders found in the manual prepared by Matthew answers that Jesus provided.

A Gospel for the Church

Matthew is the only Gospel that indicates that Jesus ever spoke of "the church." When Peter acknowledged that Jesus is the Messiah, Jesus replied with a blessing for Peter and with the promise to build His church: "Blessed are you, Simon son of Jonah . . . . And I tell you that you are Peter [which means 'rock'], and on this rock I will build my church, and the gates of Hades will not overcome it" (Matt. 16:17,18). Here Jesus states clearly His intention to form a church, and He identifies Himself as its builder. The reference to Peter has to do with his confession of Jesus. Whenever Jesus is confessed to be the Messiah, the Son of the living God, Jesus builds His church. Apart from this confession, the church does not exist.

Because Jesus spoke of building His church on a rock, it is common to imagine the church as an impregnable fortress. What Jesus actually had in mind was an army on the march whose progress could not be halted even by the gates of hell. Jesus remains the builder and Lord of the church, who leads His people in a triumphal procession among the nations.

On another occasion Jesus described the church as believers gathered for church discipline. He was addressing the matter of sin within the congregation: "If your brother sins against you, go and show him his fault, just between the two of you. If he listens to you, you have won your brother over. But if he will not listen, take one or two others along, so that 'every matter may be established by the testimony of two or three witnesses.' If he refuses to listen to them, tell it *to the church;* and if he refuses to listen even to the church, treat him as you would a pagan or a tax collector" (18:15-17, italics added). Verses 18-20 instruct the church to pray with the assurance that the effectiveness of their prayer depends not upon numbers but on the presence of Jesus with them (18:18-20).

One example of Matthew's distinctive orientation toward life in the church is provided by his use of Jesus' parable of the lost sheep (18:10-14). It is very interesting to discover that a similar parable is recorded by the evangelist Luke as well (Luke 15:4-7). The context of the parable in Luke is *evangelistic*. Jesus told the parable because the Pharisees and the teachers of the law were complaining that He welcomed sinners (Luke 15:2). In the parable, the lost sheep who is found is a sinner who is *added* to the church (Luke 15:7). But in Matthew the context concerns *church discipline*. Jesus speaks of "one of these little ones who believes in me," who is led into sin (Matt. 18:6). A "little one" is a disciple who already belongs to the church because he believes in Jesus. In the parable that Jesus told, the lost sheep is thus one who is *restored* to the church because God "is not willing that any of these little ones should be lost" (Matt. 18:14). This difference in emphasis needs to be appreciated, for it indicates that Matthew intended to prepare a Gospel for the church.

Christmas and Easter

One reason for Matthew's popularity, from its own day to the present, is its account of the Christmas story. Mark began his Gospel abruptly with the appearance of John the Baptist and Jesus of Nazareth, who came to John to be baptized (Mark 1:1-11). Not one word was devoted to the circumstances surrounding Jesus' birth or His earlier years in Nazareth. Matthew supplied what Mark was lacking. Christians who are familiar with the Christmas story know that some details were preserved by Matthew and others by Luke. But they are not always careful to remember which of the details are taken from each of the two accounts. The birth narratives in the two Gospels can be kept apart once the distinctive emphasis of each writer is seen. Matthew emphasized:

1. Disclosure through dreams (1:20-24; 2:12,13,14, 19-22)
2. The telling of the story from Joseph's perspective (1:18-25; 2:13-15, 19-23)
3. Herod the Great (2:1-8,12,16-19,22)
4. Wise men (Magi) and the star (2:1,2, 7-12)
5. The flight into Egypt (2:13-15,19,20)
6. The slaughter of the children at Bethlehem (2:16-18)

Luke, on the other hand, emphasized:

1. Disclosure through angels (Luke 1:11-20, 26-38; 2:8-14)
2. The telling of the story from Mary's perspective (1:26-58; 2:4-7, 16-19, 34, 35, 48)
3. Caesar Augustus (2:1-3)
4. Shepherds in the fields (2:8-20)
5. The presentation of the infant at the Temple (2:21-40)
6. The youth of 12 at the Temple (2:41-52)

Matthew was particularly interested in the fulfillment of ancient prophecy in the birth of Jesus (Matt. 1:22,23; 2:5,6,17,18,23).

Balancing Matthew's interest in the Christmas story was his interest in the events surrounding Easter. Mark concluded his Gospel as abruptly as it had begun, with the account of the empty tomb and the word of instruction conveyed by the divine messenger (Mark 16:1-8). He had not included (according to reliable early manuscripts), any of the resurrection appearances of Jesus. Here again Matthew supplied what could not be found in Mark. He reported the meeting between Jesus and the women who had come to the tomb on Easter morning, when Jesus confirmed that His disciples would see Him in Galilee (Matt. 28:8-10). He then briefly sketched the actual reunion, when Jesus gave to His followers the Great Commission to "disciple the nations" (28:16-20).

In writing of Christmas and Easter Matthew spoke of worship. The Magi from the east sought out the newborn King of the Jews in order to worship Him (2:1,2,11). On a similar note, the 11 disciples went to Galilee, and when they saw the risen Lord "they worshiped him" (28:16,17). By framing his Gospel with the accounts of Christmas and Easter, and by stressing the note of worship, Matthew expresses his understanding of evangelism and the extension of blessing for the nations as acts of worship which honor the Lord of the church.

3
A Defense of the Faith
Luke-Acts

A Single Work in Two Volumes

Those who first read the two-volume work prepared by the Gentile, Luke, a Christian physician and companion to the apostle Paul (Col. 4:14; 2 Tim. 4:11), recognized that it was different from other Gospels in at least two respects.

First, it told the story of Jesus with full awareness that Rome dominated the world. The birth of Jesus, for example, took place under circumstances dictated by an imperial decree issued by Octavian, better known as Caesar Augustus (Luke 2:1-7). The ministry of John the Baptist, which served to thrust Jesus before Israel, began in the fifteenth year of Octavian's successor, Tiberius Caesar (Luke 3:1). In the second volume Luke spoke of a famine in Judea which occurred while Claudius was emperor (Acts 11:28). Jewish leaders from the church in Rome could be found in Corinth because of a decree issued by Claudius (Acts 18:1,2). The "Caesar" to whom Paul appealed as a Roman citizen who had been denied justice (Acts 25:11,12,21; 26:32; 27:23,24), was the emperor Nero. Of all the evangelists, Luke alone makes mention of the Roman emperors. This feature of Luke's work would not escape the notice of his patron, Theophilus, a Roman official who appears to have held the rank of governor (Luke 1:3; Acts 1:1).

The second feature which set Luke's writing apart from other Gospels was the fact that it extended the story of Jesus to include the story of the early church in its expansion from Jerusalem to Rome. An account of the growth of the church was no afterthought which motivated Luke to pick up his pen a second time once he had completed the Gospel. He had planned from the beginning to include the material which now fills his second volume. His Gospel would trace the story of Jesus from the circumstances surrounding His birth, youth, and public ministry in the Roman province of Judea to the period of His exaltation as Lord when the church had taken root throughout the empire. It is appropriate, therefore, to speak of Luke-Acts, a single work in two volumes or, to be more accurate, one long account committed to two rolls of papyrus of nearly equal length.

Unfortunately, in the decades following the age of the apostles the two rolls became separated. The codex, or book, replaced the roll as a more convenient form for church use because several documents could be brought together in a single book. It was natural for the first roll of Luke's work to be copied alongside other works that told the story of Jesus. In this way a Gospel collection was formed. Once this occurred, the unity of Luke's two-volume work was easily forgotten. The second roll was separated from the first and was regarded as an independent work, the book of Acts. The rediscovery that Luke-Acts is a single document in two volumes permits a fresh appreciation of Luke's intention and achievement.

Luke the Historian

If Paul had not spoken of Luke as a medical doctor (Col. 4:14), it would have been easy to believe that he was a professional historian. He was obviously familiar with the historian's craft. The use of a formal prologue stating the occasion for writing, the sources of the information, the personal involvement of the writer, and the purpose of his work (Luke 1:1-4) would be recognized by any educated Jew or Gentile as the distinguishing mark of a work of history. The impression created by Luke's opening lines would only be confirmed by the formal manner in which key events are dated (Luke 2:1,2; 3:1,2). Reference to the ruling emperor and to the provincial governor was a standard practice in historical writing. The brief summary of the content of the first volume in the preface to the second (Acts 1:1,2) was entirely in the manner of the histories of Greece and Rome which had been published in that period. Luke approached his task as a historian. He holds the distinction of being the first historian of the early Christian movement.

Being aware that Luke planned and wrote his two volumes as a unified whole becomes important at this point. In early historical work, the formal prologue always served to introduce the *entire* account. It was placed as a preface to the first volume but it was written with an awareness of any other volume that was to be included within the work. That means that Luke 1:1-4 is the introduction not only to the Gospel of Luke, but to the Acts as well.

The occasion for writing Luke-Acts was the circulation of other accounts of early Christian origins (Luke 1:1). The sources of the material in *both* volumes were primarily oral, as Luke drew upon the accounts of those who were eyewitnesses and ministers of the word (Luke 1:2). Luke's involvement was not limited to historical research. When he claims to have personally investigated everything carefully from the beginning (Luke 1:3) he is anticipating the well-known "we" and "us" sections of the Acts—16:10-16; 20:5,6; 21:1-17; 27:1—28:16—where the use of the first person plural indicates Luke's own participation in certain of the events. The intention that Theophilus may know the certainty of the things he had been taught (Luke 1:4) extends not only to the story of Jesus but to that of the church as well. Luke 1:1-4 is the formal prologue to Luke-Acts.

Works of history frequently spilled over into more than one roll of papyrus. The reason for this was practical. Rolls were made by sewing sheets of papyrus together. But if a roll exceeded 30 feet, it had a tendency to break. Historians therefore planned their works in units of 30 feet or less! One estimate is that the Gospel of Luke would fill up 31 feet of papyrus, and the Acts another 28 feet. Luke carefully planned his history in terms of two rolls of papyrus. Following the standard practice of other historians, he attached a preface to the second roll which referred in a general way to what he had already written. The purpose of that preface was to indicate that the second roll continued the account presented in the first.

The second preface actually extends for several lines (Acts 1:1-5). The contents of the first roll are quickly summarized in terms of "all that Jesus began to do and to teach" until His ascension (Acts 1:1,2; Luke 24:50,51). The remaining lines are devoted to details which had occupied Luke's attention in the closing section of his Gospel: the convincing proof that Jesus was alive following His crucifixion and burial, Luke 24:13-43; His continuing ministry to the apostolic company, Luke 24:36-48; and the command not to leave Jerusalem until the Holy Spirit promised by the Father had been received, Luke 24:49. In this manner Luke provides a smooth transition between the two parts of his work.

Although Luke did not give a title to his history, it is

not difficult to discover one with which he would have been pleased. The description of the first volume as "all that Jesus began to do and to teach" (Acts 1:1) implies that the second volume sustains the account of what Jesus is doing and teaching, only now through the agency of the apostles and others who came to faith in the early days of the church. The history that Luke prepared for Theophilus and for the church could thus be entitled "The Acts of Jesus."

Luke the Apologist

In the ancient world a document which was prepared as a defense against incriminating charges was known as an apology, and its author as an apologist. Although Luke gave to his work the form of a history, the purpose of Luke-Acts was apologetic. It defended the early Christian movement from the charge that Christian commitment and Roman concerns were incompatible at a time when Roman officials were beginning to regard the Christian movement with suspicion.

Luke's strong apologetic concern explains why he chose to set the story of Jesus and the church within a frame of reference provided by the Roman situation. It also accounts for the strong concentration in the Gospel of Luke upon the innocence of Jesus. Mark and Matthew had referred to the pre-trial hearing held by the Sanhedrin which led to Jesus' trial before Pilate. But only Luke mentions a third hearing before Herod Antipas, the ruler of Galilee, as well (Luke 23:6-12). The importance of this new piece of information is clear: both Pilate and Herod agreed on the innocence of Jesus (Luke 23:4,14,15,22). In fact, Pilate had three times pronounced Jesus to be innocent and the charges against Him unfounded. Although the Roman governor finally gave in to the pressure of the crowd's demand for the death penalty (Luke 23:16-25), the issue of Jesus' innocence was kept alive when one of the criminals who was crucified with Him declared, "This man has done nothing wrong" (Luke 23:41).

Luke's keen interest in this repeated testimony to Jesus' innocence is evident in the climax to the account of the crucifixion. According to the tradition preserved by Mark and Matthew, the Roman centurion in charge of the executions had recognized Jesus as the Son of God (Mark 15:39; Matt. 27:54). But Luke records that "when the centurion saw what had taken place, he praised God and said, 'Certainly this man was innocent!' " (Luke 23:47, *RSV*).

Although Jesus had been condemned to death by a Roman court of law and had been crucified as a common criminal, He had violated no law and had posed no threat to Rome. This was an important point that Luke wished to underscore for Theophilus and for any other Roman official who had been instructed to investigate the possible threat to Roman concerns represented by Christians throughout the empire.

In the second volume Luke sketched the spread of the Christian movement from Jerusalem westward to Rome. The goal of his account is already anticipated in the commission given the disciples to be witnesses to Jesus "to the ends of the earth" (Acts 1:8). Luke understood this phrase to mean Rome, the limits of the west. There is a note of finality near the end of the account when the arrival of Paul and his party is announced with the words, "And so we went to Rome" (Acts 28:14). Between Jerusalem and Rome, Luke traced the response to the preaching of the gospel in Judea, Samaria, Caesarea, Antioch, across Asia Minor and into the provinces of Macedonia and Achaia in Greece.

Luke indicates his primary interest in the unfolding story of the church's advance by emphasis and repetition. The conversion of Paul, the Apostle to the Gentiles who was responsible for the establishment of churches in so many centers of the empire, is told three times (Acts 9:1-19; 22:1-21; 26:1-23). The conversion of the Roman centurion Cornelius, the first Gentile to become a Christian, is also recounted three times (Acts 10:1-48; 11:1-18; see also 15:7-11). Luke makes much of the fact that the apostle Paul was himself a Roman citizen (Acts 16:35-39; 22:23-29). It was only as a Roman citizen imprisoned in an imperial province that Paul could appeal to have his case reviewed before the emperor in Rome (Acts 25:8-12,16-21; 26:32; 28:17-19).

Throughout the account Luke shows a keen interest in the response of Roman officials to the presentation of the Christian message. Even Romans of the rank of governor had become Christians (Acts 13:6-12; 28:7-10). When Paul had been brought before Gallio, the governor of Achaia, on a variety of charges, no basis was found for legal action against him (Acts 18:12-17). Although Paul was arrested in Jerusalem and imprisoned in Caesarea for an extended period of time, the Roman officials familiar with the details of his case knew he had been falsely detained (Acts 23:29; 24:22-27; 25:24-27; 26:32). The favorable judgment on the innocence of Paul complements the insistence on the innocence of Jesus in Luke's first volume.

The final scene has Paul under house arrest in Rome. But the freedom that he enjoyed to preach and to teach "without hindrance" (Acts 28:30,31) indicates that Rome saw no conflict between its own interests and the proclamation of the gospel.

By addressing his apology to Theophilus, who had already received instruction in the Christian faith (Luke 1:4), Luke hoped to answer the slander that one could not serve both Christ and the empire.

Luke's Achievement

Luke's two-volume work was an impressive achievement. His association with Paul had served to introduce him to many persons in Jerusalem, Caesarea and elsewhere who could remember what Jesus had said or done or who had participated in the dynamic events which marked the birth of the church. These were "the eyewitnesses and servants of the word" to whom Luke referred in Luke 1:2. It is possible that Luke began to collect the material now found in Luke-Acts as proof of the innocence of Paul on the supposition that the Apostle would be brought to trial in Rome and information would be needed concerning the roots of the Christian movement.

One of the accounts of Christian origins that came into his hands was the Gospel of Mark, and Luke made extensive use of this source. But he had available other sources as well, both oral and written. The extent of Luke's contribution to the story of Jesus can be measured when it is compared with Mark. A careful examination of the Gospel indicates that it is like Mark in the sense that it traces Jesus' ministry from Galilee through Perea and Judea to Jerusalem. But at two major points Luke includes information not found in any other Gospel.

Luke inserts into Mark's outline of the Galilean ministry a block of teaching which extends from Luke 6:20—8:3. His major contribution, however, occurs in his account of Jesus' teaching ministry in Perea and Judea. Mark covers this phase of Jesus' ministry with a single chapter (Mark 10:1-52). Luke devoted 10 chapters to this phase (Luke 9:51—19:27), and almost all of this section is not found elsewhere. The material preserved only by Luke extends from Luke 9:51—18:14, and is known as Luke's "great insertion" in Mark's outline. This block of material contains many of the best known parables of Jesus, including the Good Samaritan, the Prodigal Son, the Rich Man and Lazarus, and the Unjust Judge. If Luke had not preserved this teaching, the loss to the church would have been enormous.

The value of Luke's second volume, the Acts, is also difficult to overestimate. Luke's account is an invaluable source of the life and character of the early church, and his summaries of the preaching of the apostles are an important indication of the convictions of the first believers. Acts also provides an indispensable frame of reference for the missionary activity and letters of the apostle Paul. Finally, Luke-Acts provides the bridge between the life and ministry of Jesus, which takes place in a Jewish setting in Galilee and Judea, and the establishment of a church which by Luke's time was becoming increasingly Gentile in character. If Luke had not written about the Hellenists, Greek-speaking Jewish Christians who were driven out of Jerusalem and who possessed the missionary vision to close the gap between the Jewish and the Gentile world, this development would be almost incomprehensible. In Luke-Acts early Christians found a Gentile perspective disciplined by the Spirit of God.

4
A Witness to the Truth
The Gospel of John

A Distinctive Witness

Mark, Matthew, and Luke are called the Synoptic Gospels because they share the same outline for telling the story of Jesus. The word *synoptic* means that they see the course of events in Jesus' life in a common way. Each of them traces Jesus' ministry from the time of His entrance into Galilee, following John's imprisonment, to His decision to go to Jerusalem where He met His death and was resurrected. The summary of one of Peter's sermons (Acts 10:37-42) indicates that the source of this outline was early Christian preaching. Although each of the Synoptic Gospels has its own emphases and distinguishing marks, they share much in common.

The reader of John's Gospel finds himself in touch with a distinctive witness to Jesus which has little in common with the Gospels prepared by the Synoptic evangelists. Over 90 percent of the fourth Gospel is not found in the other three. The first task for a student of John is to begin to grasp some of the distinctive features of John's Gospel.

Only John reports the early Judean ministry of Jesus. He devotes chapters 1—3 to a period in Jesus' life, not mentioned by the other evangelists, during which Jesus moved freely between Judea (see, for example, John 1:19-42; 2:13—4:2) and Galilee (see, for example, 1:43—2:12).

The popular response to Jesus' early Galilean ministry reported by the other Gospels reflected the fact that Jesus was already well known: "When he arrived in Galilee, the Galileans welcomed him. They had seen all that he had done in Jerusalem at the Passover Feast, for they also had been there" (4:45). From that point forward Jesus labors in Jerusalem (see 5:1-47; 7:2—10:42) as well as in Galilee (see 4:46-54; 6:1—7:1).

If the church possessed only the Synoptic Gospels, it would have been thought that Jesus went to Jerusalem on only one occasion in His adult life—to celebrate the Passover before His death. On such an understanding, it would have been possible to compress the ministry of Jesus into a period of months, or at most a year. John, however, indicates the passage of time by referring to the Jewish Passover. It is clear that Jesus' ministry extended for at least two-and-a-half years for John speaks of three Passovers: (1) Jesus is in Jerusalem for the feast (2:13,23; 4:45); (2) Jesus is in Galilee (6:1-4); (3) Jesus is again in Jerusalem (11:55,56). Jesus was in Jerusalem for other Jewish festivals as well (5:1; 7:2,10,14,37-39; 10:22,23). John's Gospel is thus an important corrective to the impression conveyed by the Synoptics that Jesus' ministry lasted only for a year.

Another striking feature of John's record is the openness with which Jesus speaks about Himself. In the Synoptic Gospels Jesus shows a reluctance to have others know who He is. To a man with leprosy whom He had cured Jesus says, "See that you don't tell this to anyone" (Mark 1:44). When persons possessed by evil spirits were crying out, "You are the Son of God," Jesus "gave them strict orders not to tell who he was" (Mark 3:12). When Peter finally recognized that Jesus was the Messiah, Jesus warned His disciples not to tell anyone about Him (Mark 8:29,30).

But in the Gospel of John Jesus is the Revealer, and He speaks openly about His identity and mission. When a Samaritan woman with whom Jesus was speaking said, "I know that Messiah . . . is coming. When he comes, he will explain everything to us," Jesus openly declared, "I who speak to you am he" (John 4:25,26).

Moreover, it is John who records the words of Jesus when He described Himself as the bread of life (John 6:35,41,48,51). or the light of the world (8:12; 9:5), or as the good shepherd who lays down His life (10:11-18). The restraint imposed by Jesus upon the open disclosure of His identity in the Synoptic Gospels appears to be relaxed in John.

Another major difference between the Synoptic Gospels and John is evident in the treatment of the teachings of Jesus. In the Synoptics Jesus' teaching generally consists of short, provocative statements which develop a single point. Even larger units, like the Sermon on the Mount (Matt. 5:1—7:27), are made up of a series of brief statements as Jesus turns from one subject to another. But in the fourth Gospel Jesus is allowed to develop His teaching with long speeches.

It is particularly striking that Jesus' teaching is frequently related to His acts of power. Jesus' feeding of the 5,000 is reported in all four Gospels, but only in John does Jesus feed the multitude and the next day describe Himself as "the bread of life" in a heated discussion with certain Jews in the synagogue in Capernaum (John 6:1-59). This is typical of John's witness to Jesus. Jesus'

teaching that He is the light of the world is verified when
He opens the eyes of a blind man who had lived in
darkness from his birth (John 8:12—9:41). Jesus proclaims that He is the resurrection and the life, and His
words take on profound meaning when Lazarus is raised
from the dead (John 11:17-44). The correlation between
Jesus' words and His deeds is one of the most characteristic elements in John's witness to Jesus.

Finally, a person familiar with the gospel story from
the Synoptics is surprised to find the omission of certain
features which one would expect to find in a Gospel. But
at every point, he discovers that for these omissions John
has substituted other material not found in the Synoptic
Gospels. A partial list of these omissions and substitu-
tions may be helpful.

• *The birth narratives,* familiar from Matthew and Luke,
are missisng in John. But John begins his Gospel by
speaking of the Incarnation, when God became flesh and
appeared among men (John 1:1-18).

• One of the most familiar features of Jesus' teaching in
the Synoptics is *His use of parables*. There is not one
parable in John but there is an abundance of carefully
developed imagery (John 10:1-18).

• In the Synoptics it is common to find collections of
Jesus' commandments, like the Sermon on the Mount
(Matt. 5:1—7:23) or the Sermon on the Plain (Luke
6:17-49). In John there is an emphasis upon the keeping of
Jesus' commandments (John 14:15, 21; 15:10), but these
commandments are not defined. What is defined is the
"new commandment" to love one another (John 13:34;
15:12).

• Each of the Synoptics reports the Transfiguration as a
moment of glory in which Jesus' character as God's
beloved Son was displayed before Peter, James and John.
The Transfiguration is absent from John, who stresses
that glory characterized the whole of Jesus' ministry

(John 1:14). Particularly in His mighty works, which John calls "signs," Jesus displayed His glory (2:11).

• The three Synoptic evangelists record the conversation which Jesus held with four of His disciples on the Mount of Olives. There He spoke of the tribulation which would accompany the fall of Jerusalem, which was itself a fore-shadowing of God's final judgment on the world. *John makes no reference to this block of instruction.* He does record Jesus' instruction to all of the disciples, after they had left the Upper Room (John 14:31), when Jesus spoke of the tribulation they would experience in the world (15:18-25; 16:33).

• The institution of the Lord's Supper, with Jesus' words interpreting the significance of the bread and the cup, is found in all three of the Synoptic Gospels. It would seem inconceivable that the story of Jesus could be told without this account. *Yet it is not present in John's Gospel.* John does speak of the Passover meal (John 13:1,2), but he focuses all attention upon the washing of the disciples' feet (13:3-17), and the teaching that Jesus gave to His followers in the Upper Room (13:18—14:31). It is possible that he considered Jesus' teaching on the bread of life (6:26-58) as a substitute for Jesus' word concerning the significance of the bread at the meal (Mark 14:22). Similarly, he may have regarded Jesus' description of Himself as the true vine (John 15:1-17) as a replacement for Jesus' word concerning the meaning of the cup (Mark 14:23,24). But if this is so, he has made no attempt to connect them closely with the meal itself.

• The Synoptic presentation of Jesus in Gethsemane where He prayed for the removal of the cup of God's wrath only to conclude with the words, "Yet not what I will, but what you will" (Mark 14:36), holds a firm place in any retelling of the sufferings of Jesus. John clearly knew this, for he speaks of the entry of Jesus and His disciples into an olive grove and the subsequent arrest of

Jesus (John 18:1,12). But *of Jesus' anguish or prayer in Gethsemane he says nothing*. In fact, he speaks of Jesus crossing the Kidron Valley and going to the olive grove only "when he had finished praying" (18:1), in reference to the priestly prayer offered by Jesus for Himself, for His disciples, and for all believers (17:1-26), prior to entering Gethsemane.

Although this is not an exhaustive account of the differences between John and the Synoptic Gospels, it is sufficient to establish that in the fourth Gospel the church possesses a distinctive witness to Jesus.

The Gospel of the Resurrection

What explanation can be given for the different perspective and emphasis in the Gospel of John? The evangelist provides the key to his entire Gospel in the account of Jesus' expulsion of the merchants and money-changers from the outer court of the Temple (John 2:13-16). When the Jewish leaders demanded proof of Jesus' authority to clear the Temple, He responded with the riddle, "Destroy this temple, and I will raise it again in three days" (2:19). Those who had challenged His authority understood His words in their literal sense: "The Jews replied, 'It has taken forty-six years to build this temple, and you are going to raise it in three days?' " (2:20). As far as they were concerned, that was the end to the conversation. But the evangelist then provides the needed key: "But the temple he had spoken of was his body. After he was raised from the dead, his disciples recalled what he had said. Then they believed the Scripture and the words that Jesus had spoken" (2:21,22).

No passage in the Gospel of John is more important than this one for understanding John's method. He makes it clear that when Jesus spoke of raising the temple in three days it was not only the Jewish leaders who failed to understand the meaning of His words. The disciples, including John himself, also misunderstood. Not until after Jesus' resurrection was it possible for the disciples to recall what had been said and to understand that Jesus had spoken of His body in a figurative way. By stressing the connection between Jesus' resurrection and the actual meaning of His statement, John indicates that he is writing his Gospel from a vantage point he did not himself enjoy during Jesus' earthly ministry. John puts his reader on the scene with the measure of understanding he would enjoy only after the Resurrection when the meaning of Jesus' words was demonstrated by the course of events. For this reason John may be described as the Gospel of the Resurrection.

The evangelist reminds his readers of his method in the account of what Jesus did on the final day of the Feast of Tabernacles. This festival served to remind the Jewish people of God's faithfulness to Israel during the period following the exodus when Israel was in the wilderness. Each day some new feature of Israel's past was brought before the people. On the last day of the festival the high priest appeared in one of the Temple courts carrying a jar of water which he poured upon the ground. This action was a remembrance of God's gift of water from the rock when Israel was suffering from thirst.

At the appropriate moment, Jesus stood in the assembled crowd "and said in a loud voice, 'If a man is thirsty, let him come to me and drink. Whoever believes in me, as the Scripture has said, streams of living water will flow from within him' " (John 7:37,38). The evangelist then explains the meaning of Jesus' invitation: "By this he meant the Spirit, whom those who believed in him were later to receive. Up to that time the Spirit had not been given, since Jesus had not yet been glorified" (7:39). John could not have known that Jesus was speaking about the Holy Spirit when He promised streams of living water. He received this insight only after Jesus had been "glorified,"

that is to say, after Jesus' resurrection and the conferring
of the gift of the Holy Spirit. John's reader, however, is
not kept in the dark concerning the meaning of Jesus'
utterance, because the evangelist immediately takes him
aside and instructs him. The emphasis of the fourth Gospel falls on understanding, but John makes it clear that
until Jesus had been glorified and the Spirit had been
given, Jesus' words were like a riddle which could not be
solved.

In the instruction of the disciples in the Upper Room,
Jesus had much to say concerning the Holy Spirit. One
statement deserves particular attention: "All this I have
spoken [to you] while still with you. But the Counselor,
the Holy Spirit, whom the Father will send in my name,
will teach you all things and will remind you of everything
I have said to you" (14:25,26). The key phrase in this
promise is that the Spirit will remind the disciples of
everything Jesus had said. That explains how the disciples
later *remembered* passages of Scripture which shed light
on Jesus' deeds (2:17) or the words that Jesus had spoken,
which they had promptly forgotten because they failed to
understand their meaning (2:22). John wrote his Gospel in
response to the ministry of the Holy Spirit (16:12-15).
Jesus is the Revealer in the fourth Gospel because the
reader can listen to His words with the understanding the
Holy Spirit has given. If John were to be asked, *Where
can the church find what the Spirit had declared concerning Jesus?* he would undoubtedly reply, *In the Gospel
which I have prepared and placed in your hands*.

The Beloved Disciple

Early church tradition was agreed that the fourth
evangelist was John the Apostle, the brother of James and
the son of Zebedee (Mark 1:19,20). In the pages of his
Gospel John does not refer to himself by name, but he has
been recognized as the nameless "disciple whom Jesus

loved" (John 13:23; 19:26; 20:2; 21:7,20). He was a relatively young man during Jesus' ministry, and enjoyed the position of honor at Jesus' right hand in the fellowship meals shared with the disciples (13:23; 21:20). He appears to have been the only disciple present when Jesus was crucified, and was entrusted with the care of Mary, the Lord's mother (19:25-27). On Easter morning he investigated the report of Mary of Magdala that the tomb in which the body of Jesus had been laid was empty, and when John saw the evidence he believed that Jesus was alive (20:1-9). John had begun to follow Jesus in connection with a miraculous catch of fish (Luke 5:1-11), and when that miracle was repeated after Jesus' resurrection, it was John who immediately recognized the presence of the Lord (John 21:7).

When John wrote his Gospel he was no longer young. He was in fact very old, and his great age appeared to support a rumor among the Christians that Jesus had said that John would not die. On the final page of his Gospel John mentions that rumor, only to correct the false impression it had created (21:20-23). He then acknowledges his responsibility for the book he had prepared (21:24).

John was at this time in Ephesus and had responsibility for a regional network of churches that extended northward to Smyrna and Pergamum, and then eastward into the interior of the province of Asia where church centers existed in Thyatira, Sardis, Philadelphia, and Laodicea. The first years of the final decade of the first century were troubled times for the church. There were many forms of pagan worship which competed for the minds and hearts of men. John wrote to assure those who had only recently joined the church that they were correct to place their faith in Jesus as Messiah and Son of God (20:30,31).

But John also found it necessary to respond to false teaching which had surfaced in the churches. Heretical teachers declared that Jesus only *appeared* to have come in the flesh. John responded to the challenge of those who denied that the Son of God had come in the flesh with the stirring affirmation that "the Word became flesh and lived for a while among us. We have seen his glory, the glory of the one and only Son, who came from the Father, full of grace and truth" (1:14). God had made Himself visible in breathtaking fashion; He had taken human flesh as the man Jesus of Nazareth in order that men and women might know Him and receive life through His name. In the closing paragraph of the Gospel the apostle brings together his own testimony and that of the church as a final word of assurance (21:24). Still vigorous as a pastoral leader of the churches in his old age, John prepared his Gospel as a witness to the truth.

5
Mission and Church Nurture
First and Second Thessalonians

Mission to Thessalonica

When Paul, Silas, and Timothy left Philippi they traveled westward along the Egnatian Way, a famous overland military highway that stretched across Macedonia. They did not stop at Amphipolis, the capital of the district, or at Apollonia. They were eager to reach Thessalonica, the most important and heavily populated center in Macedonia at that time.

Thessalonica was the principal seaport of the province and a naval station for the imperial fleet. Its fine harbor facilities accounted for the importance the city had gained as a center for trade and commerce. For its services to Rome in an earlier day Thessalonica had been declared a free city. Its privileged status is reflected in references to the public assembly for the conduct of civic affairs (Acts 17:5) and to the civil magistrates elected by the people

(Acts 17:6,8). The city enjoyed a reputation for strong loyalty to Rome and to the emperor. The cosmopolitan population included an established Jewish community with a synagogue. It was this feature that proved especially attractive to Paul (Acts 17:1).

Paul arrived in Thessalonica in the year 49, and remained there for about one month. During this period he supported himself and his companions through skilled labor as a weaver and through gifts received from the Christians in Philippi (1 Thess. 2:9; 2 Thess. 3:7,8; Phil. 4:16). On three successive Sabbath days Paul carried on a vigorous dialogue with his fellow Jews, establishing from the Scriptures that the Jesus who suffered and rose from the dead was the Messiah (Acts 17:2,3). This phase of the mission met with a degree of success. Some Jews, several Gentiles—who under the influence of synagogue preaching were participating in the life of the Jewish community, and some women from the wealthier families of the city joined Paul and Silas (Acts 17:4). But Paul had not limited his mission to the synagogue. He had preached in the open market and in the forum as well and had been able to persuade a considerable number of Gentiles unreached by the synagogue to abandon idolatry and to recognize the Lordship of Christ (1 Thess. 1:8-10). These former pagans, together with the believers from the synagogue, became the core of the new church.

The mission to Thessalonica came to an abrupt end by the decision of the new Christians themselves. The synagogue leaders had enlisted a crowd of rabble and had succeeded in throwing the city into an uproar. They stormed a house where the converts had gathered for instruction and dragged the owner, Jason, and some of the believers before the public assembly where the synagogue leaders accused them of treason (Acts 17:5-8). The riot was as serious a threat to the free status of the city as the charge that Paul and his party were installing Jesus as a rival to Caesar. Jason was forced to post a bond, guaranteeing that the peace of the city would not be disturbed by the presence of Paul and his companions. It is unlikely that Paul would have given his consent to this, but the agreement was made without his knowledge (Acts 17:9). When the brothers asked the missionaries to leave the city, they complied reluctantly. After elders had been appointed to provide leadership for the congregation (1 Thess. 5:12,13), Paul, Silas, and Timothy slipped away under the cover of darkness (Acts 17:10).

The Mission and Report of Timothy

Paul and his companions went next to Berea where the message they proclaimed was well received (Acts 17:10-12). But when a group of men representing the synagogue leadership in Thessalonica pursued them to Berea and openly sought to stir up antagonism toward them (Acts 17:13), the apostle knew that his departure from the city had not put an end to the violent opposition to his mission. Paul withdrew from Berea in the company of some of the believers who escorted him to Athens, but he left behind Silas and Timothy to organize the church (Acts 17:14,15).

In Athens Paul became anxious. His mission to Thessalonica had been brief and his expulsion from the city sudden. The more he thought about the new church which had been established there, the more concerned he became. Had they been given sufficient instruction? Would they be able to withstand the pressure of those who opposed them? The arrival in Berea of men from Thessalonica had made it clear that the Jewish leaders intended to continue their opposition to the new congregation.

Although Paul had been separated from his converts only a short while, he felt a strong urge to be with them (1 Thess. 2:17,18; 3:10,11). His inability to return was frustrating ("Satan stopped us," 1 Thess. 2:18), and the lack of news unsettled him. As soon as Timothy arrived in Athens from Berea Paul delegated him to return to Thessalonica to learn what was happening (1 Thess. 3:1-5). Paul left Athens shortly for Corinth, where Timothy later rejoined him (Acts 18:5; 1 Thess. 3:6).

Timothy's report greatly encouraged the apostle (1 Thess. 3:6-10). The Thessalonians were maturing in faith and love. Moreover, they were as eager to see Paul as he was to be reunited with them. In spite of hardships, they remained firmly committed to their new faith. Persecution in the form of derision and harassment from their fellow citizens (1 Thess. 2:14) had not deterred them.

The sobering news concerning the relentless efforts of the synagogue leaders to undermine Paul's mission was not unexpected. They had openly questioned the apostle's integrity. They contended that his religious appeal had been grounded in error. They labeled his gospel as human delusion. They compared Paul to one of those roving charlatans who arrived on the scene intending to exploit the people. They insinuated that Paul had no genuine concern for those who had responded to his preaching. They also implied that the enthusiasm generated by Paul's gospel encouraged impurity and other excesses.

The mission and report of Timothy was the immediate occasion for Paul's earliest letter. Then, as now, a letter was a substitute for a visit. Writing was just one step removed from speaking. It permitted a conversation to be sustained through the exchange of greetings and news. A letter turned absence into presence. Although Paul could not return to Thessalonica he could "visit" with the church through his written word. First Thessalonians demonstrated the value of a letter for advancing the Christian mission and provided a method, which Paul would employ for the remainder of his ministry, for maintaining contact with the churches.

First Thessalonians: Paul's Apology

Paul's concern was to respond to Timothy's report. His profound thanksgiving for the Thessalonians' faith is evident in his review of the mission to Thessalonica (1 Thess. 1:2-10). As Paul recalls the course of events he touches on several matters on which he will expand in the body of the letter: the power of the Spirit demonstrated in his preaching (v. 5); the integrity displayed in the lives of the missionaries (v. 5); the strong faith evident in the response of the believers (vv. 6-9); and the firm persuasion of Christ's glorious return (v. 10).

The tone of the opening paragraph is warm and confident, reflecting the assurances Paul had received from Timothy that the mission had not been in vain. That tone, however, is not sustained. The business at hand was to respond to the attacks of the synagogue leaders who had disputed the integrity of Paul's message, his motives, and his conduct. The charges leveled against him were serious and demanded a response. The first half of the body of the letter is devoted to this matter (2:1—3:13). It can be designated Paul's apology, for here the apostle defends the character of his ministry at Thessalonica and the integrity of his concern for the Thessalonian believers after his departure.

Paul's assertions are emphatic: "You know, brothers, that our visit to you was not a failure. . . . For the appeal we make does not spring from error or impure motives, nor are we trying to trick you. . . . You know we never used flattery, nor did we put on a mask to cover up greed—God is our witness" (2:1, 3, 5). These statements are characteristic of this section and indicative of Paul's forthright response to his detractors. He and his colleagues had spoken "as men approved by God to be entrusted with the gospel" (2:4). His message was not an expression of human cleverness but "the word of God," and its divine character was demonstrated by the quality of life it produced in the believers (2:13-15).

Paul emphatically denies that the source of his appeal was "impure motives." His intention had been not "to please men, but God who tests our hearts" (2:3,4). He flatly rejected the use of flattery to attain his purposes. He had been motivated neither by greed nor by the desire for praise (2:5,6), but by love (2:7,9). That love was evident in the openness with which the missionaries had shared their lives with the Thessalonians (2:8). It now motivated Paul's earnest prayers that he might yet return to Thessalonica and continue his ministry there (3:10,11).

In regard to his conduct, Paul builds a solid defense on the testimony of his readers: "You are witnesses, and so is God, of how holy, righteous and blameless we were among you who believed" (2:10). The gentleness he had displayed was "like a mother caring for her little children" (2:7). In matters of behavior he had adopted the stance of a father, using encouragement, warning, and exhortation to assist his children to lead a life worthy of God (2:11,12). Paul's prayer that the believers might be presented to God "holy, righteous and blameless" would have been pointless if he had failed to regulate his own conduct by the same high standard he had established for them.

The Weak, the Idle, and the Timid

Paul's earnest desire to see the Thessalonians again was motivated by his concern to supply what was lacking in their faith (3:10). Timothy had observed specific areas in which the congregation was experiencing difficulties. An important clue to this more negative aspect in his report is provided near the close of the letter when Paul identifies three groups who required sustained attention: "And we urge you, brothers, warn *those who are idle*, encourage *the timid*, help *the weak*, be patient with everyone" (5:14, italics added). Paul would have worked with these groups personally if he could have been present. Unable to return to the city, he used the final segment of his letter (4:1—5:11) to engage in the ministries of warning, encouragement, and helping. What he wrote was prompted by the failures of "the weak," the irresponsible conduct of the "idle," and the fears of "the timid."

Sexual immorality marred the conduct of "the weak." Their failure to understand that consecration to the living God was moral as well as religious identifies this group as former pagans who had come to faith (1:9,10). Hellenistic society was essentially amoral and sexual behavior was considered a matter of indifference. Although Paul had instructed these converts from paganism concerning the moral implications of faith in Christ (4:6), they had not broken old attitudes and practices. Paul, therefore, renews his ministry to them in 4:2-8: a Christian is to "avoid sexual immorality"; he is to "learn to control his own body"; and he is not to violate another person. God's will is that believers are to be holy.

The group designated "the idle" must have been recognized by Paul even before he left Thessalonica, for he had laid down the rule, "If a man will not work, he shall not eat" (2 Thess. 3:10). Disregarding this clear instruction, the idle refused to work. Their irresponsibility was aggravated by their expectation that they would be supported by the community. When support was refused on the ground of Paul's ruling, the idle had accused the church of a breakdown in brotherly love. Their behavior had disrupted the peace of the church and invited the disrespect of outsiders, and Paul warns them to change their attitude (1 Thess. 4:9-12).

The fears of "the timid" were perhaps a normal response when some members of the fellowship died. Death was a frightening reality in the ancient world. The inscriptions on gravestones along the road reminded travelers of the finality of the grave. But Paul had brought a message of hope based on Jesus' resurrection and the assurance that He would return for His people (1 Thess. 1:9,10; 2:19,20; 3:13; 5:23,24). Did the death of Christians mean that his message was mistaken? Would death exclude them from a share in the triumphant climax to history? The church had been given insufficient instruction on this matter. Paul rectified this with the encouragement offered in 4:13-18. God will raise those believers "who have fallen asleep" and they will take their place among those who will escort the Lord to earth at His coming.

The timid were also afraid that they would be unprepared for the awesome "day of the Lord" when God comes to judge everyone. Paul reassures them that their fears are unfounded: "For God did not appoint us to suffer wrath but to receive salvation through our Lord Jesus Christ. He died for us so that, whether we are awake or asleep, we may live together with him" (5:9,10). The day of the Lord is a day of wrath, but not for God's redeemed people. Paul calls the timid to engage in the ministry of encouragement he had extended to them (5:11).

Second Thessalonians: A New Crisis

A few weeks after Paul sent his first letter to the church he found it necessary to write again. He learned from a visitor or a letter that the congregation required his direction. Some of the brothers were persuaded that Paul had said that the day of the Lord had already come (2 Thess. 2:1,2). Their certainty about this alarmed the timid, for it meant that no time remained to acquire the blamelessness upon which Paul had insisted in his first letter (1 Thess. 3:13; 5:8). They were convinced that the wrath reserved for unbelievers would engulf Christians as well!

The idle, on the other hand, had rejected Paul's instruction and continued to embarrass the church. Paul wrote 2 Thessalonians in response to this new crisis. The letter is devoted almost entirely to the practical encouragement of the fearful Christians he had addressed in his previous letter (2 Thess. 1:3—3:5) and to the discipline of the idle (3:6—15).

The apostle's intention was not to introduce new insights but to remind the congregation of instruction he had already given them (2:5; 3:10). Paul was a pastor whose first concern was to strengthen the confidence of the believers. The vivid reference to the last judgment is introduced to assure the Thessalonians that they will be included among the number of those who make up God's holy people (1:6-10). The rapid sketch of the events which lead to the consummation of history and the coming of the Lord (2:3-12) is provided so that the community cannot be deceived by some prophecy, report, or letter which proves to be false. Paul insists that believers have been destined by God to share life and fellowship with Him (1:5-7,11,12; 2:1,13-17; 3:1-5). This was the encouragement the timid needed to receive.

The discipline of the idle is made the responsibility of the majority in the church (3:6-15). They are not to associate with anyone who rejects the tradition Paul had delivered orally or in writing (2:15; 3:6,10,14). The purpose of the discipline of separation is to make the offender ashamed of his actions. Yet Paul cautions the church to exercise discipline in the spirit of love, not regarding a Christian who refuses to work as an enemy, but warning him as a brother (3:15).

6
CONFUSION AND CRISIS
First and Second Corinthians

Mission to Corinth

The vision of planting the church on Greek soil brought Paul to Corinth, a prosperous commercial center situated on a causeway between two seas. The city controlled the land route between north and south and provided a land link in the sea route between east and west. It was served by two fine harbors, Cenchreae on the Aegean side of the isthmus, and Lechaeum on the Adriatic. Nearly all shipping made use of these ports because sailing around the tip of the Greek peninsula was extremely hazardous due to severe weather. Sea captains could unload their passengers and cargo at one port, knowing that another ship would be waiting for them. Travelers and commerce from every part of the civilized world moved overland from sea to sea through Corinth.

When Paul entered Corinth in A.D. 50 the city was less than 100 years old. The old city had been destroyed in 146 B.C. as punishment for military opposition to invading

Roman forces, and for a century the site was unoccupied. Julius Caesar, however, recognized the strategic importance of the location and determined to rebuild Corinth as a Roman colony. Within two years the work had advanced sufficiently to permit repopulation. The new city experienced phenomenal growth and became the fourth largest city in the empire. Designated the capital of the Roman province of Achaia and the administrative seat for southern Greece, it enjoyed a reputation as a thriving center.

Corinth was known for its pleasures and vice. "To Corinthianize" was polite Greek for "to practice immorality"; "a Corinthian girl" was a prostitute. The city boasted the only amphitheater in Greece. Its numerous theaters, baths, taverns, and shops catered to every taste. As an "open" city whose only tradition was the pursuit of profit and pleasure, Corinth attracted an unstable, transient population. A confusing variety of Oriental and Hellenistic religious cults were represented by temples, shrines, and altars. In Corinth, the melting pot of Achaia, Paul encountered the empire in miniature.

At Philippi, Thessalonica, Berea, and Athens a pattern of penetration, opposition, and withdrawal characterized Paul's mission. He successfully penetrated these centers with the gospel and churches were established. But each time strong opposition had forced Paul to withdraw after a relatively brief ministry. In Corinth, however, the pattern was altered. Paul penetrated the city, encountered stiff opposition, and nevertheless established residence there for 18 months (Acts 18:1-11). Four factors encouraged Paul to remain in Corinth.

First, soon after his arrival he met Aquila and Priscilla. They had been expelled from Rome by an imperial edict together with other Jewish-Christian leaders, and had only recently come to Corinth. Like Paul, they were tentmakers and they extended the hospitality of their home to the apostle (Acts 18:1–3). So harmonious was this arrangement that when Paul left Corinth for Ephesus he took Aquila and Priscilla with him (Acts 18:18). They were with him during the more than two years he labored in Ephesus (Acts 19:8-10; 20:31).

The second factor that encouraged Paul to remain in Corinth was that when Silas and Timothy came from Macedonia to rejoin Paul in Corinth they brought a gift of money from Philippi. This made it possible for Paul to devote himself exclusively to the ministry of preaching (2 Cor. 11:9; Phil. 4:15,16; Acts 18:5).

The third factor was supernatural in character. When Paul encountered the opposition of synagogue leaders (Acts 18:6) he was strengthened by a vision in which God instructed him to keep on speaking. The pledge of God's presence and protection was directly responsible for Paul's determination to remain in Corinth (Acts 18:9-11).

The fourth factor was an economic as well as a spiritual one. Corinth administered the games held every two years at Isthmia, the ancient sanctuary of Poseidon, less than 10 miles to the south of the city. These games attracted large numbers of delegates, athletes, merchants, and visitors from Europe and Asia. The Isthmian games were held in the spring of A.D. 51 while Paul was still in Corinth. A vivid passage in 1 Corinthians, in which the apostle describes himself as God's athlete, suggests he had been present at the games (1 Cor. 9:24-27). In April or early May when the games were held, the air is chilly and there can be violent gusts of wind and frequent showers in the region. Shelter is imperative, and Paul and his companions would find a ready market for the tents they produced during the preceding months. Also, those who became Christians at the games would carry the gospel to cities and towns Paul had never visited.

When Paul left Corinth, the church was well established, and was meeting next door to the synagogue in the house of Titius Justus, a godly Gentile (Acts 18:7). Among its local leadership were Crispus and Sosthenes, prominent members of the Jewish community who had been elected officials of the synagogue (Acts 18:8, 17; 1 Cor. 1:1, 14). After Paul left the city, another Jewish-Christian leader, Apollos, who was gifted in public debate, came to Corinth and ministered there (Acts -18:27,28).

First Corinthians: Confusion at Corinth

During an extended stay in Ephesus (A.D. 52-55) Paul kept in touch with the Corinthians through an exchange of letters and delegates. He was aware that there was confusion at Corinth over a perplexing variety of issues. An earlier letter, written in response to a report concerning sexual immorality within the congregation, has not been preserved. The report may have come from members of Chloe's household (1 Cor. 1:11), who apparently kept Paul informed on conditions in Corinth. Paul had written "not to associate with sexually immoral people," but he found it necessary to take the matter up again in 1 Corinthians because his intention was misunderstood (1 Cor. 5:9-13).

At the time Paul wrote his second letter to the church, 1 Corinthians, he had received new information from three sources. The first source, members of Chloe's household, informed him of the bickering and division in the church. The congregation was breaking up into small groups which boasted about the merits of their favorite teachers and their wisdom (1 Cor. 1:10-12). They regarded Paul, Apollos, Cephas, and even Christ as wisdom teachers, similar to popular speakers who traveled from place to place, winning a following through their eloquence and the cleverness of their proposals for successful living. Such comparisons indicated gross misunderstanding. Christian teachers are not competitors in a contest based on oratorical skills, but stewards of God who are accountable to Him (1 Cor. 3:3-9; 4:1-5). The gospel is not Hellenistic wisdom. The proclamation of the cross of Christ offends both Jews and Greeks, although to men of faith it displays the power and wisdom of God (1 Cor. 1:18-25; 3:18-21). The Corinthians are not to be identified with the wise of this world, for they are immature and without wisdom (1 Cor. 1:26-28; 2:6—3:3). Paul responds to the report from Chloe's household in 1 Corinthians 1:10—4:21.

A second source of information was the three-man delegation appointed by the church to deliver a letter to Paul (1 Cor. 16:17,18). From Stephanas, Fortunatus and Achaicus the apostle learned of confusion at Corinth involving a case of incest (1 Cor. 5:1,2), lawsuits among church members (1 Cor. 6:1), and sexual immorality (1 Cor. 6:12,13). His strong reaction is recorded in 1 Corinthians 5:1—6:20.

A third source of information was the letter from the church leaders which indicated confusion on a number of other matters. The several issues are sufficiently indicated by Paul's introductory phrase "now about" (1 Cor. 7:1, 25; 8:1; 12:1; 16:1, 12) as he takes up the questions contained in the letter from the church. The Corinthians had asked about marriage (7:1-24) and the unmarried state (7:25-40), food offered to idols (8:1—11:1), worship (11:2—14:40), the resurrection of believers (15:1-58), and the collection for the Christians in Jerusalem who were suffering from a famine (16:1-4). Paul's replies to the letter extend from 1 Cor. 7:1—16:12.

Paul would have preferred to convey his response to the confusion at Corinth in person. His letter was simply a substitute for his presence until he could be with them (1 Cor. 16:4-5). He informed the Corinthians that he would eventually come and that they should be prepared for his arrival (1 Cor. 4:18-21; 16:5-7). Until then, he was dele-

gating Timothy to represent him (1 Cor. 4:17; 16:10,11).
The letter, which was written in the spring of A.D. 55 close
to the time of Passover (1 Cor. 5:7,8; 16:8), was delivered
by Stephanas and his companions when they returned to
Corinth (1 Cor. 16:17), presumably by ship. Timothy was
sent to Corinth by the overland route, through Macedonia. Paul was frankly anxious about the reception his
young associate would receive from the unruly Corinthians and he had hoped to prevent any adverse reaction
by arranging for the delivery of his letter several weeks
prior to Timothy's arrival.

A Third Letter: Response to Crisis

Continued anxiety appears to have motivated Paul's
sudden decision to go to Corinth himself. His arrival was
unexpected and caught the Corinthians unprepared for an
apostolic visit. What Paul learned confirmed the accuracy
of the reports he had received. It also indicated that the
church had failed to act upon the pastoral direction he had
provided in 1 Corinthians. He sternly warned the church
to correct its faults (2 Cor. 13:2) and then left the city.
Certain arrogant members of the congregation were persuaded that Paul's departure was a display of weakness
(2 Cor. 10:1,2, 10) and that his warning could be disre-
garded. In reflecting about the course of events, Paul
describes his second visit to Corinth as painful in character (2 Cor. 2:1).

Not long afterward Timothy arrived in Corinth only to
be treated with contempt. The church was still feeling the
sting of Paul's rebuke and one member of the congregation thought it was time to indicate how he felt. Timothy
was "injured" (2 Cor. 7:12), but the action was actually
aimed at Paul. When Timothy returned to Ephesus and
reported what had happened, the apostle wrote a letter to
Corinth so severe in character that he wept as he wrote it
(2 Cor. 2:4). The letter has not been preserved, but its

content can be estimated from Paul's references to the letter in 2 Corinthians 2:2-11 and 7:8-13. It was clearly an ultimatum to punish the one who had injured Timothy and to demonstrate an acceptable repentance or to expect divine judgment.

Paul's third letter to Corinth was not an idle threat. Some individuals in the church had already experienced sickness and death as a result of abuses at the Lord's Supper (1 Cor. 11:27-30). Paul had taught the Corinthians that the basis of Christian life was God's action in establishing the new covenant by the death of Christ (1 Cor. 11:23-26; 2 Cor. 3:6). The enjoyment of the blessings of the covenant depended upon obedience to God but disobedience and rebellion invite divine judgment (2 Cor. 10:1-11; 13:2-10). Paul and Timothy had come to Corinth as the commissioned representatives of the Lord (1 Cor. 16:10,11). Consequently, contempt shown for them was ultimately a display of contempt for the Lord. The seriousness of the situation exposed the whole congregation to the threat of extermination.

Paul entrusted the delivery of the severe letter to Titus, who appears to have been more confident in his authority than Timothy. He instructed Titus to remain in Corinth until the response of the congregation was known, and then to travel northward overland through Macedonia, finally rejoining Paul in Troas.

At the prearranged time the apostle arrived in Troas, but when he failed to find Titus he sailed for Macedonia (2 Cor. 2:12,13). Paul was understandably anxious to learn the outcome of his deputy's mission (2 Cor. 7:5). When he finally met up with Titus he received the report that the Corinthians desired to be reconciled to him. They had punished the offender who had injured Timothy and were eager to clear up any implication that they had been involved in showing contempt for Paul (2 Cor. 2:5,6; 7:11). Paul was overjoyed; he experienced the ministry of

God who comforts those who have been overwhelmed with grief (2 Cor. 1:3-11; 7:6,7).

Second Corinthians: Problems Unresolved

The report of Titus was the occasion for Paul's fourth letter to Corinth, 2 Corinthians. It expresses the apostle's profound relief that God will not have to destroy a congregation that he had been instrumental in establishing.

In response to the report of Titus (2 Cor. 1—7), Paul gives free expression to his joy. But the letter alternates between outbursts of relief (2 Cor. 1:3-7; 2:14-17) and frank recognition that complaints had been made against the apostle by the congregation. The almost poetic celebration of "the God of all comfort" in 1:3-11, for example, is followed by a clear explanation why Paul had not returned to Corinth after his second visit (1:15—2:1). Paul defends his integrity in response to the charge that his statements could not be trusted. This is characteristic of 2 Corinthians, a letter that reveals the depths of affliction and anguish, of joy and grief, of comfort and affliction that Paul experienced in his relationship with the Corinthians.

Paul was now prepared to come to Corinth a third time (2 Cor. 12:14; 13:1). A primary purpose of his fourth letter was to prepare the church to address a number of problems that remained unresolved. Corinth had made a commitment to participate in the collection for Jerusalem more than a year ago, but had done little to advance the project (2 Cor. 8:1—9:15). Aggravating the delicate situation in Corinth were certain traveling Jewish leaders who had recently arrived and had been received enthusiastically by the congregation (2 Cor. 10:12—12:13). They had demanded and received financial support. Paul saw them as exploiters, and with biting sarcasm labels them the "super-apostles" (2 Cor. 11:5; 12:11). The irony of the situation was that while the Corinthians welcomed these newcomers—even though they were "false apostles, deceitful workmen, masquerading as apostles of Christ" (2 Cor. 11:13)—they had ridiculed and attacked Paul. Paul contrasts with them a self-portrait of the true apostle, scarred from affliction and weakness (2 Cor. 4:10). Unable to boast of honor or power, he is, like his Lord, a suffering and dying figure who realizes triumph only in the experience of infirmity and defeat (2 Cor. 2:14-16; 4:7-12; 6:4-10; 11:23-29; 12:7-12).

Finally, Paul knew that when he came to Corinth it would be necessary to deal with the persisting problems of arrogance and immorality (2 Cor. 12:20.21).

The seriousness of these congregational problems accounts for the severity in Paul's tone in the conclusion of his letter (2 Cor. 12:19—13:10). The Corinthians' response to this letter would determine whether Paul would express the gentleness of Christ or the harshness of apostolic discipline when he revisited Corinth for the third time (2 Cor. 10:1; 13:9-11).

7
THE TRUTH OF THE GOSPEL
Galatians

Mission to Galatia

Acting upon the direction of the Holy Spirit, the leadership of the church of Antioch in Syria had commissioned Barnabas and Paul for missionary service (Acts 13:1-4). Their initial field of endeavor was Cyprus (Acts 13:5-12), but then the two missionaries sailed north by northwest to the mainland of Asia Minor, arriving at the port of Side. They passed through Perga, the chief city of Pamphylia (Acts 13:13), and from there struck inland into the highlands in the south of the Roman province of Galatia. Their destination was Pisidian Antioch, situated on a plateau some 3,600 feet high, about 100 miles or more north of Perga (Acts 13:14).

The two men appear to have made this strenuous journey to the highland region so that Paul might recuperate after he became sick in the lowlands of Pamphylia. One suggestion is that he had contracted malaria. He reminds the Galatians that "it was because of an illness" that he had first preached the gospel to them (Gal. 4:13).

Antioch of Pisidia was the chief civil and military center for southern Galatia, and a Roman colony. There was a large Jewish population resident in the city. An opportunity for evangelism was presented when Paul and Barnabas were invited by the governing body of the synagogue to address the congregation (Acts 13:14,15). The summary of the message delivered by Paul (Acts 13:16-41) indicates the way in which the gospel was proclaimed to a synagogue audience comprised of Jews and God-fearing Gentiles. The recital of the saving acts of God, from the exodus until the time of David (Acts 13:17-22), prepared the congregation for the presentation of Jesus as the Saviour promised to Israel in the Scriptures (Acts 13:23-37). The promise of the forgiveness of sins through Jesus (Acts 13:38) was supported by the assurance that "through him everyone who believes is justified from everything you could not be justified from by the law of Moses" (Acts 13:39). Paul was evidently already formulating the doctrine of justification by faith which would receive its mature expression in Galatians and Romans.

There was broad interest in Paul's message, especially among the devout Gentiles in the congregation. They apparently spread the news among their fellow Gentiles, for a week later there were more Gentiles than Jews in attendance at the synagogue service (Acts 13:42-44). This angered the leaders of the Jewish community who resorted to abuse to prevent Paul from using the synagogue as a base for evangelism (v. 45). Paul and Barnabas were ultimately expelled from the region, but not before many Gentiles had accepted the message of salvation through faith in Christ which they had proclaimed. These new Christians formed the first of the churches of Galatia (Acts 13:46-52).

The missionaries turned next to Iconium, nearly 90 miles east by southeast from Pisidian Antioch, and an important commercial center and road junction. In spite of strong opposition from Jewish leaders they were able to remain in Iconium longer, and the presentation of the gospel was confirmed by miracles. As a result, a strong Christian community was established.

The apostolic preaching caused deep division in the city. When a plot to stone Paul and Barnabas was uncovered they fled across the regional border to the Lycaonian cities of Lystra and Derbe (Acts 14:1-7).

Lystra, which was located 18 miles south by southwest from Iconium, had also been made a Roman colony by Augustus. It was linked to Antioch of Pisidia by a military road which bypassed Iconium. There were some Jewish residents in the city with whom the missionaries came in contact, among them the mother and grandmother of Timothy (Acts 16:1,2; see also 2 Tim. 1:5). Undoubtedly, the gospel was also shared with the Roman citizens of the colony as well as with the native Lycaonians.

The one incident recorded by Luke exposes the difficulties that could be encountered during a mission to a pagan center. A man who was lame from birth and who had never walked was healed. An excited crowd of native Lycaonians, who had witnessed the healing, became convinced that Zeus, the chief of the gods, and Hermes his messenger were visiting the city in human form. Inscriptions and legend demonstrate that these two Greek gods were closely associated in the worship of the people in the vicinity of Lystra. A stone altar found near Lystra, for example, is dedicated to the "Hearer of Prayer [presumably Zeus] and Hermes."

An old legend, which would have been known to every child in Lystra, told of a visit that Zeus and Hermes had once made to the city, disguised in human form. When hospitality was refused to them, the city was destroyed.[2] In their excitement the crowd reverted to the old Lycaonian dialect which the missionaries did not understand. If Zeus and Hermes had now returned, the tragic failure to recognize and honor them must not be repeated! The local priest of Zeus was summoned and appropriate sacrifices were hastily prepared to honor the two visitors. When Paul and Barnabas finally realized what was happening they were horrified and were barely able to restrain the crowd from offering sacrifices to them (Acts 14:8-18).

The refusal of the sacrifices undoubtedly offended the native population. When Jewish leaders arrived from Antioch and Iconium it was not difficult for them to turn public opinion against the missionaries. In the ensuing riot Paul was stoned and dragged outside the city in the conviction that he was dead (Acts 14:19,20). Although he had only been stunned it was not the sort of experience he could forget. Years later Paul related to the Corinthians that once he had been stoned (2 Cor. 11:25), and in his final letter to Timothy, Paul recalled his Galatian experiences again: "You know . . . what kinds of things happened to me in Antioch, Iconium, and Lystra, the persecutions I endured. Yet the Lord rescued me from all of them" (2 Tim. 3:10,11). In his letter to the Galatians Paul reminded his readers that he bore on his body "the marks of Jesus" (Gal. 6:17) in reference to the scars he had incurred from his ill-treatment at Lystra.

The final center evangelized by Paul and Barnabas was Derbe, about 60 miles southwest of Lystra. When a strong church had been established, the missionaries retraced their steps, returning to Lystra, Iconium, and Pisidian Antioch to encourage the believers and to recognize officially those who were displaying qualities of leadership within the church (Acts 14:21-23). Paul's letter to "the churches in Galatia" (Gal. 1:2), written some years later, was addressed to these four predominantly Gentile congregations in southern Galatia.

Paul returned to Galatia on at least two other occasions. On a second missionary journey, Paul and Silas followed a land route through the province of Syria and Cilicia, and then entered into the territory of southern Galatia, stopping at Derbe, Lystra, and Iconium (Acts 15:41—16:5). On this return visit Timothy began his long and fruitful association with Paul. The statement that "Paul and his companions traveled thoughout the region of Phrygia and Galatia" (Acts 16:6) implies a visit to the Christians in Antioch of Pisidia as well.

The apostle apparently followed this same overland route at the beginning of his third missionary journey. Luke records that he set out from Antioch in Syria and "traveled from place to place throughout the region of Galatia and Phrygia, strengthening all the disciples" (Acts 18:23). It was apparently during this period of ministry that Gaius of Derbe was delegated to accompany Paul. When Paul returned to Jerusalem with the love-gift from the Gentile churches the presence of Gaius of Derbe and Timothy of Lystra (Acts 20:4) provided ample testimony that the grace of God had been extended to the Galatians.

Crisis in Galatia

It may have been from Gaius that Paul learned of the crisis in the Galatian churches. Jewish-Christian teachers had arrived and were disrupting the faith of many of the believers in the four centers. They asserted that Gentiles could not become Christians unless they first became full converts to Judaism. They insisted upon the necessity of circumcision and the importance of zeal for the Mosaic law.

Paul had already encountered this "Judaizing" position in Antioch shortly after the establishment of the churches of Galatia. He and Barnabas had become involved in a bitter debate with some men from Judea who were teaching that salvation depended upon the accept-

ance of circumcision (Acts 15:1). When the matter was
submitted to church leaders in Jerusalem for consideration, former Pharisees who had come to faith stated cate-
gorically: "The Gentiles must be circumcised and required to obey the law of Moses" (Acts 15:5).

On that occasion the leaders from Jerusalem had supported Gentile freedom (Acts 15:13-29). Now, several
years later (A.D. 56), Judaizing teachers were seeking to
reopen the issue, claiming the full support of the leadership of the church in Jerusalem. They disputed Paul's
version of the gospel and sought to discredit his authority
as an apostle. Their statements about Paul and his gospel
can be reconstructed from the apostle's fiery response in
Galatians, which was written from Ephesus in the white
heat of the controversy. Paul responded sharply because
he understood that the teaching of the Judaizers entailed a
fundamental denial of the gospel of grace and of his own
integrity.

The first impression a reader of Galatians receives is
conveyed by the tone of the letter. The opening lines
indicate that Paul is bristling with indignation. The qual-
ification that his apostleship was "not from men nor by
man, but by Jesus Christ and God the Father, who raised
him from the dead" (Gal. 1:1), is a categorical denial that
Paul owed his apostleship to the action of the Jerusalem
apostles, or perhaps to Peter or to James as the Judaizers
claimed. This expanded address prepares for the elaborate
defense of his apostleship in the body of the letter where
Paul insists that he was commissioned by God, not by
men (see especially 1:15—2:10).

Paul similarly expands the greeting section of the
letter with a capsule summary of the gospel he preached
(Gal. 1:3-5). His reason for doing so is that the Judaizers
implied that Paul withheld from the Galatians crucial
elements in the gospel, namely, the demand for circumcision and the necessity of zeal for the law. The body of the

letter is primarily a response to this charge. The absence of any statement of thanksgiving is striking. In this respect Galatians differs from all of Paul's other letters to the churches. The acceptance of the teaching of the Judaizers was so serious there could be no statement of thanksgiving.

The body begins abruptly with a statement of astonishment which brings before the Galatian Christians the central issue of the gospel and its perversion (1:6,7). Paul is emphatic: there is no other gospel than the message he had proclaimed and which they had accepted (1:8,9). There could not be any other gospel since the gospel Paul preached " is not something that man made up" but the truth received "by revelation from Jesus Christ" (1:11,12).

Paul was able to demonstrate that the Judaizers did not have the support of James and the apostles in Jerusalem. He refers to a private conference in Jerusalem at which he presented to James, Peter, and John the gospel that he preached among the Gentiles (2:1,2). Titus, a Gentile, was with him on this visit, and some Jewish Christians had insisted that Titus needed to be circumcised (2:3,4). Paul recognized that what was at stake was "the truth of the gospel" (2:5) and refused to comply with their demand. If circumcision had actually been an element in the gospel as the Judaizers claimed, Paul would have been opposed by the Jerusalem leaders. On the contrary, "those who seemed to be important . . . added nothing to my message" (2:6) and extended "the right hand of fellowship" to the apostle (2:9).

In support of their position, the Judaizers had also appealed to Peter's action in Antioch where he refused to share table fellowship with uncircumcised Gentiles. They undoubtedly added that Barnabas, who was well known to the Galatians, had stood with Peter. Paul takes up this incident in order to place it in its proper theological perspective for the Galatians (2:11-21). Although the matter for discussion had been circumcision in Jerusalem and table fellowship in Antioch, the deeper issue on both occasions concerned "the truth of the gospel" (2:5,14). Paul refused to compromise on this issue.

Paul's anguish that the Galatians should exchange the blessings of the gospel for a piety based upon human performance finds full expression in the impassioned outburst, "You foolish Galatians! Who has bewitched you? Before your very eyes Jesus Christ was clearly portrayed as crucified" (3:1). In this context Paul reminds his readers that through faith in the finished work of Christ they had received the blessing of Abraham. That was demonstrated when they received the Holy Spirit (3:2-14). In point of fact, the law can add nothing to the status conferred through faith in God's promise; they are already sons of God (3:15—4:7). This assurance furnishes the basis for Paul's direct appeal not to return to bondage (4:8—5:1).

The stern warning that submission to the Judaizer's demand for circumcision will invalidate what Christ has done for them (5:2-12) is not empty rhetoric. It draws its force from the fact that reliance upon the law and human performance (circumcision and the works of the law) is necessarily a refusal of the grace of God expressed in the cross of Christ. Paul brings the whole argument to a decisive conclusion that in redemption what matters is not circumcision nor uncircumcision, but "a new creation" (6:15), which can only be the achievement of God. Consequently, for the Galatians and for all Christians everywhere, "the only thing that counts is faith expressing itself through love" (5:6). There can be no agreement between the performance piety of the Judaizers and the gospel of the grace of God expressed to men in the cross of Christ (2:19-21).

8
COMMITMENT TO MISSION
Romans

Roman Christianity

It is not known how Christianity was brought to Rome. There is no evidence that the church was founded by an apostle. When Paul first arrived in Puteoli, the port city of Rome, he found Christians who were eager to extend hospitality to him, who apparently accompanied him on his journey to the capital. There he was met by still another group of believers who had come out to meet him (Acts 28:13-15).

It is possible that the church owed its beginning to Jews and converts to Judaism from Rome who were visiting Jerusalem for the festival of Pentecost in the early thirties (Acts 2:10,11). Those who may have become Christians in response to Peter's preaching (Acts 2:41; 4:4) would have returned to share their faith with others. Italians stationed militarily in Caesarea had also come to faith quite early (Acts 10:1-48), and it can be presumed that they brought Christianity with them when they re-

turned to Rome. In any event, by the time Paul wrote his
letter to the Romans the vitality of the Christian movement in Rome was well known (Rom. 1:8). The number
of believers was sufficiently large to warrant the forma-
tion of several house-churches (Rom. 16:3-5, 11, 14, 15).

Both Christian and pagan sources agree that the
church in Rome was originally Jewish-Christian in character. A fourth-century commentator on the letters of Paul
who possessed a good sense of history wrote: "It is established that there were Jews living in Rome in the time of
the apostles and that those Jews who had believed [in
Christ] passed on to the Romans the tradition that they
ought to profess Christ but keep the law. . . . One ought
not to condemn the Romans, but to praise their faith,
because without seeing any signs or miracles and without
seeing any of the apostles, they nevertheless accepted
faith in Christ, although according to a Jewish rite."[3] This
statement is consistent with the proposal that Roman Jews
and converts to Judaism who had become Christians when
visiting Jerusalem returned to share their convictions with
others in the capital.

There was a very large Jewish community in Rome. In
63 B.C. the Roman military governor of Syria, Pompey,
had intervened in Jewish affairs, laid siege to Jerusalem,
and captured it. Jews who were brought to Rome as slaves
on that occasion were later granted freedom and formed a
colony in the city. The Jewish character of early Roman
Christianity is evident in the acknowledgment of Jesus as
the Messiah and the observance of the Mosaic law.

A pagan biographer of the emperors, writing in the
early second century, offers an independent witness to the
Jewish character of Roman Christianity. Commenting
upon the fifth year of Claudius's reign (A.D. 49), he states:
"Since the Jews constantly made disturbances at the in-
stigation of Chrestus he [Claudius] expelled them from
Rome."[4] The name *Chrestus,* which means "the good

one," was rather common. But in this case it is almost certainly a garbled form of *Christus,* or "Christ." Suetonius identified Chrestus as an agitator who was responsible for the disorders in the Jewish community.

But fresh light is thrown on the situation by another brief allusion to this incident. Aquila and Priscilla are introduced by Luke as Jews who had recently come from Rome to Corinth "because Claudius had ordered all the Jews to leave Rome" (Acts 18:1,2). Evidently by A.D. 49, the church was vigorously engaged in the task of evangelizing the Jewish quarters in Rome. Heated debates over the claim that Jesus of Nazareth was the Messiah of Jewish hopes resulted in riots that brought upon the community the unfavorable attention of the emperor. The "Jews" who were expelled from Rome were apparently church leaders like Aquila and Priscilla. The action of Claudius underscores the predominantly Jewish-Christian character of the church in Rome until the time of the expulsion.

A decree of expulsion remained in force so long as the emperor was alive. Claudius died in A.D. 54. That meant that for a five-year period (A.D. 49-54) the Jewish Christians who had determined the character of the church were absent from the city. Leadership necessarily passed to Gentile Christians.

Over the course of months and years significant changes in the expression of the faith of the church and the focus of its mission inevitably took place. There was now no reason for a strong emphasis upon the Mosiac law. Gentile perspectives replaced Jewish ones in the formulation of the confessional creeds and hymns used in public worship. The evangelism of the Jewish quarters was abandoned for a mission within the forum and market where Gentiles congregated.

When Jewish Christians began to return to Rome after Claudius's death, as did Aquila and Priscilla (Rom.

16:3,4), they discovered disturbing changes in the character and missionary concern of the church. It was predictable that serious tensions would develop between Gentile Christians and Jewish Christians within the church at Rome.

Missionary Vision

Paul had long desired to visit the Christians in Rome but apostolic responsibilities in the east had prevented him from coming (Rom. 1:10-13; 15:19-22). After a lengthy period of residence in Ephesus he felt the time was ripe to extend his mission activity to the west, and for Paul that inevitably meant Rome (Rom. 1:15).

It was first necessary to complete the collection project which the apostle hoped would demonstrate the unity of the Gentile and Jewish branches of the church, and that required a trip to Jerusalem. After that, nothing would prevent him from setting out for the imperial capital. Although Paul was understandably concerned about his reception in Jerusalem (Rom. 15:25-33), he felt confident that he would soon be able to minister to the Christians in Rome. Paul wrote Romans from Corinth (Rom. 16:1,2,23) in the year A.D. 56 to prepare the church for his coming.

In the opening "thanksgiving" section of his letters Paul commonly indicated his reason for writing. Paul's statement in Romans (1:8-12) stresses his strong desire to come to Rome (1:10,11) in order that both they and he may be mutually encouraged by each other's faith (1:12). The body, or "message" section of the letter opens on the same note: Paul had often intended to come to Rome but until now had been prevented from doing so (1:13). These statements, however, remain general and naturally raise two questions in the mind of the reader: First, what prevented Paul from coming to Rome earlier? and Second, how may the Romans encourage Paul?

These questions are unanswered until the close of the body section of the letter when Paul returns to them and takes them up in the same order. Writing about his apostolic ministry to the Gentiles (15:14-18) he continues: "So from Jerusalem all the way around to Illyricum, I have fully proclaimed the gospel of Christ. It has always been my ambition to preach the gospel where Christ was not known, so that I would not be building on someone else's foundation. . . . This is why I have often been hindered from coming to you" (15:19-22).

What prevented Paul from coming to Rome was missionary activity in the east. He then goes on to say: "But now that there is no more place for me to work in these regions, and since I have been longing for many years to see you, I plan to do so when I go to Spain. I hope to visit you while passing through and to have you assist me on my journey there, after I have enjoyed your company for a while" (15:23,24).

The Christians in Rome may encourage Paul by making it possible for him to take the gospel to the Iberian peninsula, which was commonly regarded as "the limits of the west" or "the ends of the earth." Their assistance would include financial support for the mission, prayer, and perhaps the appointment of two or more men to accompany Paul to Spain.

By framing his letter with these implied questions and the answers supplied in the closing section of the body, Paul brings everything which he has to say in Romans within a missionary perspective. Paul wrote to Rome at this time because (1) he is convinced his mission activity in the east is completed, and (2) he is eager to turn his energies toward the west. This inevitably meant Rome (Rom. 1:15; 15:23,24), but for Paul it means the projection of a mission to Spain (15:24, 28). It is the mission to Spain that is the immediate occasion for the letter. The missionary character of the occasion accounts for the missionary structure which Paul gave to his letter. From this point of view, Romans is an open letter concerning missionary vision. Paul desires the Christians in Rome to share in the missionary vision which motivates him (15:23,24,28).

Justification by Faith

From his long association with Aquila and Priscilla Paul knew of the disruption of the church in Rome under Claudius (Rom. 16:3,4; Acts 18:1-3, 18,19). He later learned of the strained relationship between the Gentile Christian leadership of the church and the returning Jewish Christians. One purpose of his letter was to seek to relieve the tension between the two groups. He knew that at the time he wrote the congregation was predominantly Gentile in character, and he assumed that the church fell within the sphere of his missionary responsibilities since he was the Apostle to the Gentiles. He writes: "I planned many times to come to you . . . in order that I might have a harvest among you, just as I have had among the other Gentiles" (Rom. 1:13). But Paul envisioned a church in which Jews and Gentiles would worship together (1:16; 3:29,30; 10:12,13; 11:11-32), displaying that God had met the needs of both in a common way through Christ.

Paul's teaching on justification by faith is his pastoral response to a divided church. It is striking that in Romans every passage which speaks of righteousness or justification occurs within a larger context discussing the situation of Jews and Gentiles (1:17; 2:13; 3:4,21-26,28; 4:2,3,9; 5:1,9, 12-19; 8:30-33; 9:30; 10:3,4,6,10).

Paul was concerned to answer the disturbing question: How is it possible for the Jew and the Gentile to stand on the same level of advantage before God? Historically, the Jews had enjoyed a privileged relationship with God (3:1,2; 9:4,5). Unfortunately, that did not keep them from disobedience (2:17-25). Paul shows that at the point of personal need, there is no difference between the Jew and the Gentile. All men have rebelled against God and stand condemned before Him (1:18—3:20). Consequently, it is necessary for God to take the initiative and to put both the Jew and the Gentile in the right through His reconciling action (3:21-26; 5:6-11). God met their common need through Jesus Christ, demonstrating that He Himself is righteous and that He "justifies the man who has faith in Jesus" (3:26). The argument is theologically significant. Yet it remains intensely pastoral and practical. Justification by faith is the teaching of a missionary who reflected on the problem of sin and righteousness within the context of a church consisting of Jews and Gentiles.

Working with the category of justification by faith, it is possible to construct a useful outline of Paul's thought in Romans:

I. Paul's commitment to mission (1:1-17)
  A. The need for justification by faith (1:18—3:20)
  B. The scope of justification by faith (3:21—8:39)
  C. The historical experience of justification by faith (9:1—11:36)
  D. The evidence of justification by faith (12:1—15:13)
II. Paul's commitment to mission (15:14-33)

The value of this outline is that it demonstrates that in Romans the exposition of justification by faith does not occur for its own sake but is the response of a missionary to an important issue in the life of the church: How can Jewish Christians and Gentile Christians live harmoniously together in one church? That question had crucial bearing upon the success of the Christian mission, and it received from Paul a missionary response.

Paul concludes his exposition of justification by faith with a prayer for congregational unity and the pointed appeal to welcome one another as the only valid response to the truth proclaimed in the gospel: "May the God who gives endurance and encouragement give you a spirit of unity among yourselves as you follow Christ Jesus, so that with one heart and mouth you may glorify the God and Father of our Lord Jesus Christ.

"Accept one another, then, just as Christ accepted you, in order to bring praise to God. For I tell you that Christ has become a servant to the Jews on behalf of God's truth, to confirm the promises made to the patriarchs so that the Gentiles may glorify God for his mercy" (15:5-9).

God intends both Jews and Gentiles to come together as a community marked by praise and harmony through Christ (15:9-13). That is why they must "accept one another" (15:7). The theology of Romans, and especially the sustained concern with Jews and Gentiles, reflects the specific problem of strained relationships in the church of Rome.

9
Mandate for Maturity
Colossians; Philemon; Ephesians

Colossae—The Lycus River Valley

The Lycus River valley in the old Phrygian region of
Asia Minor was the ancient highway from the west to the
east. A major Roman road followed the contours of the
Maeander River valley for 100 miles from Ephesus to
Laodicea on the Lycus River, a tributary of the Maeander.
The road then turned southeast to follow the Lycus valley
toward Pisidian Antioch, Iconium, and through the Cili-
cian gates to Tarsus. The three major cities of the Lycus
Valley in the Roman period were Laodicea, Hierapolis,
and Colossae. Although the prominence of Colossae had
been overshadowed by its important and wealthy neigh-
bors in the first century, it maintained its status as a city
and was one of the active centers of the textile industry in
the district.

The person responsible for introducing Christianity to
the Lycus Valley was Epaphras, a native of Colossae

(Col. 4:12). It was from him that the Colossians had first learned of the gospel (Col. 1:6,7), and he had succeeded in establishing churches in Laodicea and Hierapolis as well (Col. 4:13). He had apparently become a Christian during the extended period when Paul was laboring in Ephesus, teaching daily in a rented lecture hall. Luke remarks that "this went on for two years, so that all the Jews and Greeks who lived in the province of Asia heard the word of the Lord" (Acts 19:10).

Ephesus, as the major city of Asia, attracted visitors from throughout the province. Those who became Paul's disciples were instructed by him and then returned to their own native cities prepared to engage in evangelism. The effectiveness of this arrangement was acknowledged even by those who opposed the gospel. One such spokesman observed that "this fellow Paul has convinced and led astray large numbers of people here in Ephesus and in practically the whole province of Asia" (Acts 19:26).

If this was how Epaphras became instructed in the faith it would explain why Paul describes him as "a faithful minister of Christ *on our behalf*" (Col. 1:7, italics added). Epaphras's preaching of the gospel at Colossae was an extension of Paul's ministry in Ephesus. The establishment of churches in the three major centers of the Lycus River valley can be assigned to the period A.D. 52-55.

False Piety

Paul may have passed through the Lycus valley on his third journey (Acts 19:1) but he had not stopped there in his eagerness to reach Ephesus. At the time he wrote his letters to the churches in the valley he had not visited any of the congregations that were later established by Epaphras (Col. 1:4, 8; 2:1). For information concerning Christianity in the Lycus valley Paul was dependent upon Epaphras.

Paul was under house arrest in Rome when Epaphras sought him out a few years later (Philem. 23). Although Epaphras was able to report spiritual progress in the church (Col. 1:3-8; 2:5), he informed Paul that the Colossians were facing danger on two fronts. Some members of the predominantly Gentile congregation (Col. 1:27; 2:13) were displaying a tendency to relapse into pagan conduct (3:5-11). Even more serious was the activity of false teachers. They were offering a spiritual program based upon rigorous self-denial and supported by slogans which threatened to confuse believers concerning the character of their salvation (2:4, 8-10). The major elements in their program can be detected from Paul's response (Col. 2:4-23).

Paul describes the false teaching as "hollow and deceptive philosophy" which drew upon human tradition and worldly principles (2:8). Judaism contributed the insistence upon circumcision (2:11), the validity of the Mosaic code (2:14), food and drink regulations and the Jewish festival calendar (2:16). A more distinctive element was the rigorous asceticism urged in the slogans "Do not handle! Do not taste! Do not touch!" (2:21) and confirmed in Paul's reference to "their harsh treatment of the body" (2:23). The false teachers were stressing fasting and severity to the body as a means of attaining mystical visions. They claimed that Christians who accepted their brand of ascetic piety would be qualified now to receive a vision of the angels worshiping God (2:18) which others would enjoy only after death. Such visions they described as "a shadow of the things that were to come" (2:17).

The attractiveness of the proposal was deceptive. It threatened to divide the church into those who were "spiritual" and those who were not. The promise of visions encouraged the members of the church to seek some personal advantage from spirituality rather than desiring the spiritual growth of the whole church. Paul warns his readers: "Do not let anyone who delights in false humility and the worship of angels disqualify you for the prize. Such a person goes into great detail about what he has seen, and his unspiritual mind puffs him up with idle notions" (2:18).

The proper response to the false teaching was a reminder of what the Colossians were already enjoying in Christ. For that reason Paul stresses that God has qualified them "to share [with the angels] in the inheritance of the saints in the kingdom of light" (1:12), and has already brought them into "the kingdom of the Son he loves" (1:13). In Christ "all the fullness of the Deity lives in bodily form," and the Colossians had been given "fullness in Christ, who is the head over every power and authority" (2:9,10). In short, Christians already enjoy what the champions of this false piety had argued was available only through a life of rigorous self-denial. Believers have already entered into the reality of life in the risen Lord (3:1-4).

Philemon—The Worth of a Single Individual

The threat to the churches in the Lycus valley was not the only problem with which Paul was wrestling when he wrote Colossians. Onesimus, a slave in the household of Philemon of Colossae, had robbed his master and fled to Rome (Philem. 11, 15, 18). As a fugitive, his plight was serious. The flight of a slave was one of the most serious offenses recognized by Roman law.

Through circumstances which are unknown, Onesimus had come into contact with Paul and had become a Christian (Philem. 10). He had remained with Paul and had proven useful to him (v. 11). Paul would have liked to have kept him in Rome, but he finally reached the decision that it was necessary to return Onesimus to the Lycus valley so that his presence in Rome might represent Philemon's desire as well as his own (vv. 12-14). The apostle wrote a tactful letter to Philemon to assure a favorable reception for Onesimus (vv. 8-17), who returned to Colossae in the company of Paul's messenger, Tychicus (Col. 4:7-9).

The letter is a model of spiritual direction and love, and provides strong evidence that concern for the churches had not caused Paul to lose sight of the worth of a single individual. He identifies himself with Onesimus in intimate terms: the slave is his son (Philem. 10), and in sending him to Philemon he presents his own heart (v. 12). In compliance with Roman law which made a father guarantee that all debts incurred by a child will be paid, Paul assures Philemon he will repay whatever Onesimus owes his master (v. 18). He does not hesitate to remind Philemon, however, that he himself owed something to Paul for the knowledge of the truth which had led to his salvation (v. 19). An opportunity to acknowledge that debt is provided in the delicate request that Philemon release Onesimus for a ministry with Paul (vv. 13,14,20,21).

Fifty years or so after Paul wrote the letter to Philemon, Ignatius, the senior pastor of the church of Antioch in Syria, wrote a letter to the Christians of Ephesus in which he spoke of their senior pastor, Onesimus. The man in question appears to be the former slave whom Paul had introduced to Christian life and service. His leadership in a major church center shows that Paul's conviction of his worth and Philemon's compliance with the apostle's request that he be released for the work of the ministry was thoroughly justified.

Ephesians—Summons to Maturity

Tychicus actually delivered three letters to the Lycus Valley, Colossians, Philemon and Ephesians. Although the conclusion that Ephesians was a letter addressed to a church center in the Lycusvalley may be surprising, it is supported by the text. Paul had worked for two-and-a-half years in Ephesus. Yet in Ephesians there are no personal greetings, and strong indications that those who received the letter did not know Paul personally. Paul had only "heard" of their faith (Eph. 1:15), even as they had only "heard" of his apostleship (3:2,4). Consequently, it is a safe conclusion that the letter was not addressed to Ephesus, and this is confirmed by the textual history of the letter. In the oldest and most reliable manuscripts, the words "in Ephesus" are not found in the salutation (1:1).

The first clue to the actual destination of the letter is the reference to Tychicus in Ephesians 6:21,22, where Paul's statement is almost identical to what he wrote in Colossians 4:7,8: Tychicus will provide personal information about Paul, supplementing what is expressed in the letter. The fact that the letters to the Colossians and to Philemon were delivered by Tychicus to the Lycus valley where Paul was not personally known, suggests that the letter now labeled "Ephesians" had the same destination.

A second clue is provided by Paul's instruction in Colossians 4:16. The apostle had sent a letter to Laodicea at the same time that he sent Colossians and he calls for an exchange of these letters. A careful comparison of Colossians and Ephesians indicates that they are, in fact, complementary letters; they expose related aspects of the same truth. Colossians presents Christ as the Head of the church (Col. 1:18; 2:19), while Ephesians develops the teaching that the church is the Body of Christ (Eph. 1:22,23; 4:15,16; 5:23,29,30). An exchange of letters would expose the Christians of the Lycus valley to these complementary statements of the truth.

Our "Ephesians" is almost certainly the letter that Paul sent to the church at Laodicea. Because a copy of the letter was left at Ephesus by Tychicus, later scribes assumed it was originally addressed to that center.

A closer relationship exists between Colossians and

Ephesians than between any two other documents in the New Testament. It has been estimated that 70 percent of Colossians is shared or reproduced in Ephesians, while 50 percent of Ephesians has a verbal parallel in Colossians. The relationship between the two letters can be represented graphically:

Ephesians

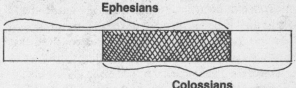

Colossians

The purpose of the two letters, however, is different. Colossians is a direct reply to the threat posed by false teaching to the churches of the Lycus valley; Ephesians is a call for reflection and maturity (Eph. 4:4-13).

The different character of Ephesians becomes clearer if attention is given to the portion of the letter which has no parallel in Colossians. The result is surprising, for when the material which is common to Colossians is removed, what remains are carefully polished units which possess a "liturgical" character. Each one is complete in itself:

- A solemn review of the redemptive ministries of God the Father, the Son, and the Holy Spirit (1:3-14)
- A confession summarizing the need for, and the experience of redemption (2:1-10)
- A prayer (3:14-21)
- A plea for church unity supported by reference to the creed and to the statement of Scripture (4:1-16)
- A plea for holy living, concluding with a portion of a hymn (5:8-14)
- An expansion of the instruction for husbands and wives, which reflects upon the relationship of Christ and the church (5:22-33)
- A warning to be prepared for spiritual conflict (6:10-17)

As a collection, these materials would be appropriate for instructing candidates for baptism. But in Ephesians they have been carefully worked into the body of the letter.

The evidence suggests that when Epaphras arrived in Rome, Paul had been working on new worship materials for the Gentile churches. He had originally intended that they be used in preparing new converts for their baptism. Reflecting on Epaphras's report, Paul recognized that these materials would be helpful in calling Christians to remember the commitment they had made to Christ at the time of their baptism. He worked these new formulations into the letter to call Christians to reflect on their previous commitment to Christ and to urge them to advance to Christian maturity as the strongest defense against the threat of false teaching (4:11-16).

The letter proved to be the key document in the New Testament on the nature and purpose of the church. God's intention is to bring all things under the headship of Christ (1:9,10,19-23). The church participates in God's plan and provides a visible expression of what God is actually doing (2:14-18). The church is God's display case where He shows not only the world but the spiritual powers who seek to disrupt the work of God that He is accomplishing what He has announced He will do. The plea to guard the unity of the church (4:1-6) and to live responsibly (4:17—6:20) follows naturally from this awesome truth. The fact that the churches participate in the accomplishment of God's redemptive plan implied the mandate for Christian maturity which Paul develops in Ephesians.

10
PARTNERS IN MISSION
Philippians

Mission to Philippi

The coming of Christianity to Philippi in A.D. 50 occurred under circumstances that were controlled by God. From Galatia Paul had intended to carry the gospel to the province of Asia, but he and his companions were prevented from engaging in a ministry there by the Holy Spirit. Turning north from Pisidian Antioch, the missionaries crossed the Sultan Dagh mountain range in the direction of Bithynia, a Roman province in northwest Asia Minor lying along the southern shore of the Black Sea.

When the Spirit denied them entrance into Bithynia, they turned westward toward Troas, a Roman colony and the normal port of call for travel between Asia and Macedonia (Acts 16:6-8). In Troas, the gateway to Europe, Paul received the direction he was seeking. He experienced a night vision in which a man was pleading, "Come over to Macedonia and help us" (Acts 16:9). Until he arrived in Troas Paul had two companions with him, Silas and Timothy; at Troas Luke joined them and indicates his presence by the use of the personal pronouns "we" and "us" in his account of their travels: "After Paul had seen the vision, *we* got ready at once to leave for Macedonia, concluding that God had called *us* to preach the gospel to them" (Acts 16:10, italics added). Luke apparently accompanied the apostle to Philippi (note Acts 16:11-17). The four men sailed directly to the island of Samothrace, and from there to Neapolis, the port city of Philippi. A short journey of eight miles inland brought them to Philippi, "a Roman colony and the leading city of that district of Macedonia" (Acts 16:12).

The mission to Philippi is summarized by Luke in a series of incidents in which the Roman associations of the city play a significant role (Acts 16:13-40). A military colony was a settlement of Roman citizens, designed to promote and protect Roman interests in a region that was predominantly non-Roman in character. There were always resident aliens in a colony who did not enjoy the privileges of citizenship but whose conduct was nevertheless regulated by Roman law. Lydia appears to have belonged to this class. She was a wealthy businesswoman from Thyatira who had established a residence in Philippi. Having come under the influence of the Jewish community in her native city, she customarily observed the Jewish Sabbath with the women of her household. The fact that there was no synagogue in Philippi indicates that there were not even 10 Jewish men within the city.

For Lydia and her women, Sabbath observance meant a service of prayer by the river beyond the city limits. Roman law stipulated that foreign cults could be practiced only outside the city gates. When Lydia and her household responded to the gospel, her house became the center for the mission to Philippi and a place for the gathering of the young church (Acts 16:13-15).

The incident involving the slave girl (Acts 16:16-18) exposes the pagan character of life in Philippi. The young woman was regarded as an oracle through whom Apollo, the Greek god of prophecy, spoke in ecstatic utterances. She was actually possessed by an evil spirit. Her practice of following the missionaries, chanting incessantly, disrupted the mission until the spirit was expelled.

When the girl was no longer able to engage in fortune-telling, her enraged owners dragged Paul and Silas before the civil magistrates. They made no mention of the girl but appealed to the anti-Semitic prejudice of the magistrates ("These men are Jews . . ." Acts 16:20), and accused the missionaries of disturbing the peace of the colony by introducing an alien religion that was incompatible with Roman citizenship (Acts 16:21).

This allegation would have been plausible only if Paul and his companions had been urging the acceptance of the gospel upon those who were citizens of the colony. The presence of a hostile crowd at the hearing (Acts 16:22) confirms that the activities of the missionaries had attracted attention prior to this incident. On the strength of the allegation Paul and Silas were turned over to the police to be beaten with rods and jailed (Acts 16:22,23; see also 2 Cor. 11:25).

The case against them was dropped the next morning when the missionaries were expelled from the city, but not before they had received an apology from the magistrates for the violation of their rights as Roman citizens (Acts 16:35-39). All citizens were protected by law from public humiliation without the benefit of a trial. The treatment of Paul and Silas is consistent with a provision in a fourth-century Roman law code for dealing with traveling seers and soothsayers: "The custom is to give them a beating and drive them out of the city."[5]

Although the imprisonment of the missionaries had led to the conversion of the jailer and his family (Acts

16:23-34), it had involved suffering. Paul recalled the incident vividly when he wrote to the Thessalonians later that year: "We had previously suffered and been insulted in Philippi, as you know" (1 Thess. 2:2).

The mission to Philippi was undertaken on Paul's second missionary journey. In the closing months of the third journey Paul passed through Macedonia on at least two occasions, and undoubtedly was refreshed by his friends at Philippi. The first occasion was prompted by his eagerness to be reunited with Titus and to learn of the response of Corinth to a letter of ultimatum he had addressed to the congregation. It was probably at Philippi that he received the report from Titus which led to the writing of 2 Corinthians (2 Cor. 7:5-7).

After a period of ministry in Corinth, Paul retraced his steps through Macedonia, *en route* to Jerusalem. This time he was accompanied by a number of men representing the churches which had participated in the collection for the saints in Jerusalem (Acts 20:4). The list included delegates from Berea and Thessalonica in Macedonia, Derbe and Lystra in Galatia, and Ephesus in Asia. The absence of a representative from Philippi is only apparent, for Luke indicates that he, and perhaps another (Acts 20:6), had been appointed to represent the Christians at Philippi in this display of the generosity of the Gentile churches.

After naming those who accompanied Paul, Luke continues: "These men went on ahead and waited for *us* at Troas. But *we* sailed from Philippi after the Feast of Unleavened Bread, and five days later joined the others at Troas, where *we* stayed seven days" (Acts 20:5,6, italics added). The reference to the Feast of Unleavened Bread identifies the time as early April, A.D. 57.

This is Luke's first indication that he had again joined Paul on his missionary journey. He stopped referring to the mission band as "us" and "we" when they left Philippi

(Acts 16:17). It indicates that when Paul left the city in the company of Silas and Timothy nearly seven years before Luke had been left behind to provide leadership for the young church. The strong supportive relationship which Paul enjoyed with the Philippians for more than a decade reflects the wholesome influence of the ministry of Luke, a Gentile.

Partnership

Paul wrote Philippians from Rome about A.D. 61 at a critical point in his life. For a period of two years he had been under house arrest, but with a relative degree of freedom which permitted him to continue his ministry of proclamation and instruction (Acts 28:30,31). This type of arrangement was designated "free custody," but it had given place to confinement, probably in the barracks of the imperial guard on the Palatine hill. Paul observes that "the whole palace guard" knew that his imprisonment was for Christ (Phil. 1:13). His trial may have begun, since the apostle speaks of his defense (1:7) and of his expectation that he will receive an acquittal (1:19,20, 25,26; 2:23,24).

The Christians at Philippi had learned of the change in Paul's circumstances, perhaps from Epaphroditus. He was a Philippian who had been appointed by the church to serve Paul during the period of house arrest (2:25,26). The Philippians were earnestly concerned for the apostle's welfare. Their anxiety was not without foundation. The emperor before whom Paul's hearing would be conducted was Nero, who had proven to be quite irresponsible in the conduct of civil affairs. If Paul were found innocent, naturally he would be released; but if he were judged to be guilty he would be consigned to flogging, exile, or capital punishment. The Philippians had no confidence that Nero would be impartial in his judgment.

Paul deeply appreciated the affection of the Philippians for him. He acknowledges that their "partnership in the gospel from the first day until now" (1:5) was a constant source of joy to him, and he openly acknowledges his own love for them (1:3-8; 4:1). One purpose that Paul had in writing to the church was to encourage them to rejoice in the Lord in spite of his uncertain circumstances, and to assure his friends that he was rejoicing in the divine superintendence of his affairs (1:8-20; 2:17,18; 3:1; 4:4).

Paul recognized that his chains had actually become an occasion for speaking about Jesus Christ to anyone who had anything to do with his case. Moreover, many of the Christians in Rome had been encouraged by Paul's example to share their faith more courageously (1:12-14). Paul's sole concern was that Christ would be exalted through him, "whether by life or by death" (1:20). He knew that God could deliver him, and this confidence is reflected in the counsel not to be anxious about anything but to rely upon the spiritual resource of prayer with thanksgiving (4:6,7).

With gentle humor, Paul conveys to the Philippians the greetings of the Christians in Rome, "especially those who belong to Caesar's household" (4:22). If God is able to place men and women of faith within the imperial palace, He is able to rescue Paul when he stands before the emperor!

Philippians, however, is more than a letter of assurance to an anxious congregation. It is also a letter of thanks, acknowledging the gifts received when Epaphroditus arrived from Philippi (4:10-18). This feature of the letter finds delicate expression already in the salutation, which can be translated, "To all the saints . . . in Philippi, together with *the [financial officers]* and deacons" (1:1, italics added). In texts relating to trade associations and pagan religious clubs in Macedonia and elsewhere, the word commonly translated "overseers" (or "bishops") designates financial officers responsible for the collection and disbursement of funds when need arose. This seems to fit the situation which Paul acknowledges in the opening and closing paragraphs of his letter.

In the initial thanksgiving section he speaks quite generally of the partnership of the Philippians in his missionary work (1:4,5). But in the closing paragraph of the body he becomes more specific: "Moreover, as you Philippians know, in the early days of your acquaintance with the gospel, when I set out from Macedonia, not one church shared with me in the matter of giving and receiving, except you only; for even when I was in Thessalonica, you sent me aid again and again when I was in need" (4:15,16).

The mission in Thessalonica, Corinth (2 Cor. 11:9), and now Rome (Phil. 4:10, 14, 18) had been supported by the generosity of the Philippians. Using a vivid expression found on commercial papyri meaning "paid in full," Paul exclaims, "*I have received full payment* and even more; I am amply supplied, now that I have received from Epaphroditus the gifts you sent" (4:18, italics added).

The presence of Epaphroditus with Paul was itself a vivid reminder of the partnership in mission which the Philippians shared with Paul. Although they could not accompany him in his travels or comfort him in his imprisonment, they could express their support of Paul's apostolic labors by delegating one of their own members to serve the apostle in any way helpful. But Epaphroditus had become severely ill and his life had been endangered. When he recovered sufficiently to travel, Paul determined to send him back to Philippi, bearing a letter containing a paragraph of commendation (2:25-30). Paul was concerned to ward off any possible criticism that Epaphroditus had not fulfilled his responsibility and had deserted Paul by returning to Macedonia.

In the commendation of this man, Paul plays upon his name, which indicates that at his birth his parents had dedicated him to the service of the goddess Aphrodite (*Ep-aphroditus* = dedicated to Aphrodite). One designation of Aphrodite was "patroness of gamblers," and the highest cast of the dice was called an *epaphroditus* because it was said that the goddess directed the hand that threw the dice. Paul develops this gambling metaphor in describing the service of Epaphroditus: "Welcome him in the Lord with great joy, and honor men like him, because he almost died for the work of Christ, *risking his life* to make up for the help you could not give me" (2:29,30). Epaphroditus had gambled with his life and won, because God was with him.

From Epaphroditus Paul had learned of the situation at Philippi. The decision that he should return to Philippi presented Paul with the opportunity to address the church on several issues. Paul used his letter to promote internal unity among the Philippians in the face of pagan harassment (1:27-30), selfish individualism (2:1-5), disturbance from Judaizers (3:2-4, 18,19), and a personal dispute between two of the leading women which had caused friction in the church (4:2,3). The paragraphs of apostolic counsel dealing with each of these matters gives to the letter the character of a pastoral directive, guiding the church to respond as men and women in Christ.

The gentleness that Paul displays in his pastoral direction is clear from his response to the two quarreling women. He does not take up the matter of their dispute until he has prepared a context of love and concern for his remarks to them. He begins to establish this context in the opening thanksgiving section of the letter, when he stresses that his prayers include all of the congregation: "In all my prayers *for all of you,* I always pray with joy *because of your partnership in the gospel* from the first day until now" (1:4,5, italics added). He prays for Euodia and he prays for Syntyche, and he remembers with joy that both women had shared in the work of the gospel (4:2,3).

When he adds, "It is right for me to feel this way about *all of you,* since I have you in my heart; for . . . *all of you* share in God's grace with me. God can testify how I long for *all of you* with the affection of Christ Jesus" (1:7,8, italics added), it is clear that Paul has chosen his words for their inclusiveness. His affection and thanksgiving extend to both women. The concern of his prayer was "that your love may abound more and more in knowledge and depth of insight" (1:9), for it was precisely a deficiency in love which permitted the quarrel to continue.

Paul's expression of his desire for the entire congregation indicates that he is thinking particularly of the two women. The instruction to conduct themselves "in a manner worthy of the gospel of Christ" (1:27) is carried forward through the development of a military metaphor. Paul wants to know that the Philippians are *stand[ing] firm in one spirit, contending [side by side as one person] for the faith of the gospel* without being frightened in any way by those who oppose you" (1:27,28, italics added). The metaphor appeals to the phalanx, a Macedonian military unit which depended upon the closest cooperation between all of the persons in the unit.

Paul returns to this metaphor when he finally addresses the quarrel. He returns to the thought of "standing firm" just before he speaks to the two women: "Therefore my brothers [and sisters], you whom I love and long for, my joy and crown, that is how *you should stand firm in the Lord,* dear friends!" (4:1). He picks up the note of contending side by side just after he has named the two women. Turning to a trusted woman in the congregation, probably Lydia, he asks for help: "Yes, and I ask you, loyal yokefellow, help these women who have *contended at my side in the cause of the gospel,* along with Clement and the rest of my fellow workers, whose names are in the book of life" (4:3, italics added). Euodia and Syntyche had taken their place in God's phalanx when the gospel first came to Philippi. Paul gently reminds them and the church that the effectiveness of the unit depends upon its close-knit harmony.

Within this context Paul finally names the two women: "I plead with Euodia and I plead with Syntyche to agree with each other in the Lord" (4:2). The appeal is direct, and is addressed to each of the women. Then the matter is dropped. Paul has no desire to embarrass the women further. His approach to this problem of strained relationships provides a model of tactfulness and love.

11
CHURCH ORDER
Titus; First and Second Timothy

Imprisonment and Release

When Paul wrote Romans (A.D. 56), his plans were to deliver the collection to Jerusalem and then to depart for Rome and Spain (Rom. 15:23-29). Those plans were frustrated when a riot in Jerusalem led to his arrest and imprisonment first in Jerusalem and then in Caesarea, the seat of administration for the Roman province of Judea (Acts 21:27-32; 22:22—23:35).

Judea was classified as an imperial province, a designation reserved for a troubled region which the emperor brought under his own supervision. The provincial governor appointed by the emperor was simply his personal representative. Consequently, any Roman citizen who felt that he had been denied justice in an imperial province could appeal to have his case brought directly before the emperor. When two years passed and a change of governors in Judea did not result in a satisfactory hearing on his situation, Paul exercised his legal right as a citizen to be sent to Rome for a trial (Acts 24:27—25:12).

When Paul arrived in Rome he was placed under house arrest for an additional two years (Acts 28:30). By the time he wrote Philippians in A.D. 61, however, some new developments had occurred. The apostle had been removed from his lodging to the barracks of the imperial guard in preparation for a hearing before Nero (Phil. 1:12-14). He was persuaded that he would either be sentenced to death or he would be released (Phil. 1:19,20; 2:17). He fully expected to be released (Phil 1:25,26; 2:24).

There was a basis for Paul's confidence in this matter. His appearance for pre-trial hearings before the provincial governors in Caesarea had demonstrated that his legal position was very favorable. No basis for capital jurisdiction had been found (Acts 23:29; 25:18,25; 26:31,32). That fact was reflected in the nature of Paul's imprisonment in Rome. Prisoners suspected of having committed crimes against the empire which were punishable by death were not granted the free custody which Paul had enjoyed for two years in the capital (Acts 28:30).

In the absence of any proven charge against him, Paul may have secured a merely casual release from Nero. This proposal is supported by the fact that the emperor had shown a measure of clemency in dealing with the lower social classes in Italy.[6]

An alternative suggestion is that the emperor had exercised his authority to shorten the court list by dropping cases long overdue for prosecution, and so had acted as Paul's benefactor. The early fourth-century church historian, Eusebius, states that Paul was in fact released: "Tradition has it that after defending himself, the Apostle was again sent on the ministry of preaching, and coming a second time to the same city [Rome], he suffered martyrdom under Nero."[7]

The letters of Titus and 1 Timothy clearly presuppose

that Paul was released from prison and engaged in further missionary activity in the eastern Mediterranean. His plans to take the gospel from Rome to Spain (Rom. 15:24,28) were apparently abandoned.

Philippians indicates that he was contemplating a return to Macedonia (Phil. 1:25,26; 2:24). Paul may have found insufficient support or actual opposition to the mission to Spain in Rome (see Phil. 1:15-18; 2:20,21). On the other hand, the decision to revisit key centers in Asia Minor and Macedonia could have been dictated by developments within the churches in those regions during the years of his absence.

Paul turned eastward, stopping first on the Mediterranean island of Crete where he conducted an evangelistic ministry in several cities (Titus 1:5). He then returned to Ephesus before passing into Macedonia (1 Tim. 1:3) where he must have visited with friends in Philippi, Thessalonica, and Berea. Gradually he made his way north to Nicopolis in Epirus where he established a residence in preparation for an extended mission (Titus 3:12). Incidental allusions in 2 Timothy (4:13,20) indicate that he had visited Corinth, Miletus, and Troas as well. It was apparently from Nicopolis that Paul penned the letter to Titus and the first of the two letters to Timothy.

Titus—Example in Crete

Paul had not remained in Crete to organize the new churches in the cities where he had preached the gospel. That task was entrusted to Titus who was left behind at Paul's departure (Titus 1:5). The letter to Titus is essentially a pastoral directive; it was written to encourage Titus in the performance of his ministry and to supplement the oral instructions he had received from Paul. The letter is filled with imperatives which indicate the range of responsibilities that had been entrusted to Titus: church leaders must be appointed (1:5-9), divisive persons must

be silenced (1:10-16; 3:9-11), and reliable instruction
must be given to the several age groups and social classes
which had responded to the gospel (2:1-6,9,10;
3:1,2,8,14). In his own actions Titus must provide an
example which the new believers can follow, and his
teaching must reflect integrity and earnestness (2:6-8).
Paul reminds his associate that his task includes both
encouragement and stern rebuke (2:15). The letter provided Titus with apostolic instruction for setting up stable
new churches in centers only recently evangelized. Paul
regarded strong leadership and godly, disciplined lives as
important sources for commending Christianity to others.

The letter also provides insight into Paul's custom of
delegating pastoral tasks to the several gifted men he had
gathered around him. The letter summons Titus to join
Paul in Nicopolis as soon as Artemas or Tychicus arrives
in Crete to relieve him of his responsibilities (3:12). He is
informed that he can anticipate the arrival of Zenas the
lawyer and of Apollos, presumably from Rome, and is
instructed to provide them with anything they may need
for the continuation of their journey (3:13). An impression is conveyed of men in motion in response to the
direction they received from Paul in the overseeing of the
churches and the advancement of the gospel.

First Timothy—Supervision in Ephesus

When Paul arrived in Ephesus he found that the
church was in urgent need of pastoral supervision. There
were controversies involving the exercise of the teaching
office (1 Tim. 1:3-11; 2:12), an acceptable standard of
Christian behavior (1:18-20; 4:2,3), and the character of
sound doctrine (4:1-5; 6:3-5). The apostle felt that it was
necessary for him to continue on to Macedonia; but before
he left he delegated Timothy to remain in Ephesus and to
assume responsibility for the overseeing of the congregation. Paul intended to return to Ephesus and to give his

personal attention to the problem of restoring order to the church. But he recognized that if he were delayed, Timothy would require both encouragement and instruction (3:14,15; 4:13). First Timothy is a pastoral directive, outlining Timothy's personal and official responsibilities in Ephesus.

When Paul wrote to Titus he was concerned with the establishment of congregations that would be able to commend Christianity to a pagan society. In his first epistle to Timothy he turns his attention to an established church in need of correction. The major threat to the congregation was coming from a class of teachers who were drawing false doctrinal implications from the Jewish law, sowing strife and dissension in the congregation, and leading morally corrupt lives (1:3-7, 18-20; 4:1-3; 6:3-5). This explains why Paul lays such stress upon "sound doctrine" (1:10; 6:3) and loyalty to the "faith" or doctrine received from the apostles (1:18,19; 2:7; 3:9; 4:1,6,16; 6:12,20,21). Paul regarded heresy as a festering disease which consumes the body of the church (2 Tim. 2:17, "Their teaching will spread like gangrene"). He compares that apostolic tradition to a valuable deposit which must be guarded (1 Tim. 6:20). His own respect for the tradition is evident from the manner in which he introduces faithful "sayings" (1:15; 3:1; 4:9) and older confessions of faith (3:16; 6:13-16) into the statement of the letter.

Paul describes the church as "a pillar and foundation of the truth" (3:15). It was the responsibility of each congregation to support and commend the gospel by its continuous witness. The members of the church must be equipped to share their faith in an attractive fashion and to defend the truth against the distortions of the false teachers. That is why Paul stresses the importance of public worship (2:1-15) and the public reading of Scripture as the basis for preaching and teaching in the congregation (4:11-16).

This practical concern for the strengthening of Christian character and witness also accounts for the amount of space devoted to men and women with a special responsibility for ministry. The list of qualities to be looked for in anyone who desires to hold church office (3:1-13), the lengthy discussion concerning an order of widows who were being supported by the church (5:3-16), and the detailing of the conditions for the discipline of an elder (5:19-21) that Paul provided for Timothy gives to 1 Timothy the appearance of a manual of church order.

Second Timothy—Come to Rome

The circumstances surrounding Paul's return to Rome are unknown. Nero's decision to persecute the Christians in Rome for a fire which destroyed much of the imperial city in A.D. 64[8] may have affected Christians in the provinces. All that can be said for certain is that Paul was arrested, that he was brought back to Rome to face trial again, and that his situation was precarious.

The conditions of his second imprisonment in Rome were far more severe than his earlier experience of custody. He was chained like a criminal (2 Tim. 1:8,16,17; 2:9). It was dangerous for anyone to be associated with him and, in at least one instance, it had cost a faithful friend his life (1:16-18). Many of Paul's acquaintances abandoned him (1:15; 4:10). The testimony of a pagan metalworker had proved damaging to him (4:14), and at his trial no one supported him (4:16). Of his many associates, only Luke remained with him. (4:11).

Although Paul's status as a citizen had been recognized and he would not be condemned to face the lions in the arena (4:17), he had been sentenced to die. He fully expected to be executed before the winter was over (4:6-8,21). Paul was prepared to die, but he was eager to see his son in the faith, Timothy, once more before he met his Lord. He wrote his final letter, 2 Timothy, urging

Timothy to come from Ephesus to Rome before travel became impossible with the winter storms (1:4; 4:9, 13,21).

The letter provides an intimate portrait of Paul. His affection for Timothy is openly expressed. When they had parted at Ephesus, Timothy had wept. That was the last time the apostle had seen the younger man, and he felt the pain of their separation: "Recalling your tears, I long to see you, so that I may be filled with joy" (1:4). Paul was stirred by the longings of a father to be reunited with a son whom he loved (1:2). His desire to see Timothy was intensified by the fact that he had been deserted by others with whom he had been close and he felt isolated in his situation (1:15; 4:10,16). He needed his young men around him: "Do your best to come to me quickly. . . . Get Mark and bring him with you, because he is helpful to me in my ministry . . . Do your best to get here before winter " (4:9,11,21).

The reference to John Mark is linked with the surprising indication that Paul continues to think in terms of his ministry (4:11). With the approach of winter he needs his cloak which he left with one of the brothers in Troas. But he also requested that Timothy bring his scrolls, and especially the parchments (4:13). The scrolls may have been papyrus copies of his correspondence, for it was customary for a letter-writer to preserve a copy of what he had written. The parchments were almost certainly leather scrolls containing portions of the Old Testament.

Paul intends to occupy himself with the care of the churches and the instruction of God's Word, even if it must be from the confinement of his cell as he awaits the day of his execution. He knew that the Roman Empire was powerless to stop the program of God: "Remember Jesus Christ, raised from the dead, descended from David. This is my gospel, for which I am suffering even to the point of being chained like a criminal. But God's word is not chained" (2:8-10). In that confidence Paul commends a life built upon the foundation of the holy Scriptures (3:14-17) and gives to Timothy the sacred charge to "preach the Word" (4:2).

Paul was familiar with the tradition of a farewell speech. He had delivered such a speech to the Ephesian elders when they had met with him at Miletus prior to his final journey to Jerusalem (Acts 20:18-35). There were three standard elements in this type of address: (1) a reminder of what the audience already knew from past associations with the speaker; (2) a charge covering present responsibilities; and (3) a warning of what would take place after the speaker's departure.

Paul gave to 2 Timothy this form of a farewell speech. He reminds Timothy of the response of prominent Christians in Ephesus to him (2 Tim. 1:15-18), and of Timothy's own knowledge of Paul (3:10,11); he charges him to remain loyal to the tradition and to fulfill his ministry (1:8,9,13,14; 2:1-8,19-26; 3:14—4:5); and he warns his associate of the godlessness which will characterize the last days (3:1-9). By casting the letter in the form of a farewell address Paul presents Timothy and the church with his last will and testament. Beyond the shadow of the executioner's axe, Paul fixed his vision upon the Lord who would receive His servant and award him the victor's crown (4:7,8).

12
ENCOURAGEMENT AND WARNING
Hebrews

An Early Christian Sermon

The placement of Hebrews among the letters of the New Testament encourages a reader to regard this document as a letter. The opening lines, however, indicate that it does not possess the form of an ordinary letter. The writer fails to identify himself or the group to whom he is writing. There is no prayer for grace and peace and no statement of thanksgiving or blessing. This document begins with a majestic sentence celebrating the dignity of the Son through whom God has spoken His final word (Heb. 1:1-4). The opening statement commands attention and involves a reader immediately. Hebrews begins like a sermon.

The accuracy of this first impression is confirmed by the writer. In brief personal remarks added at the end (13:18-25) he describes his work as a "word of exhortation": "Brothers, I urge you to bear with my word of

exhortation, for I have written to you briefly" (13:22).
This unusual description recalls the invitation extended to
Paul and Barnabas in the synagogue at Antioch of Pisidia:
"Brethren, if you have any word of exhortation for the
people, say it" (Acts 13:15, *RSV*). "Word of exhortation"
was the normal designation for the sermon which followed the readings from the Law and the Prophets in the
synagogue. The exhortation consisted of helpful encouragement and warning. This is precisely the character
of the sermon which the writer of Hebrews prepared for
his hearers.

Recognizing that Hebrews is a sermon permits important features of the style and structure to receive the
attention they deserve. The writer is concerned to convey
the impression that he is present and is actually delivering
the sermon he has prepared. He avoids reference to actions like writing and reading that would emphasize the
distance which separates him from the group he is addressing. Instead, he stresses the actions of speaking and
hearing, which are appropriate to persons in conversation,
and identifies himself with his audience in a direct way:

- "We must pay more careful attention, therefore, to what
  we have heard, so that we do not drift away" (2:1)
- "It is not to angels that he has subjected the world to
  come, about which we are speaking" (2:5)
- "We have much to say about this, but it is hard to
  explain because you [have become hard of hearing]"
  (5:11)
- "Even though we speak like this, dear friends, . . ."
  (6:9)
- "The point of what we are saying is this: . . ." (8:1)
- "But we cannot discuss these things in detail now" (9:5)
- "And what more shall I say? I do not have time to tell
  about . . ." (11:32)

The writer has used this device to diminish the sense
of the distance which separates him from his audience and

which makes writing necessary. Hebrews was prepared for delivery as a sermon to the congregation.

The writer uses literary structure to communicate effectively with his audience. He alternates between the exposition of his theme and practical application of his message.

The first thought he develops is that Jesus is superior to the angels (1:5–2:18). His interest in the angels was intensely practical. It was widely accepted in Judaism that the law of God had been delivered through the angels (Acts 7:38,53; Gal. 3:19). The Jewish Christians whom he addressed held this belief (Heb. 2:2) and found in it a strong reason for respecting the law. The exposition of Jesus' superiority to the angels (1:5-14) serves the writer's pastoral purpose by preparing for the earnest plea not to neglect the message of salvation which was delivered by Jesus (2:1-4).

The writer then resumes his exposition (2:5-18). This pattern is sustained throughout Hebrews and is characteristic of a sermon. Alternating with the encouragement provided by the writer's exposition of the high priestly ministry of the Son of God are a series of warnings covering the neglect of the message of salvation (2:1-4), the sin of unbelief (3:7—4:11), the denial of Christ (5:11—6:20), the failure to persevere in the Christian life (10:19-39), and the refusal of the God who is speaking (12:14-29). The proper way to listen to Hebrews is to recognize that it is an early Christian sermon and to come prepared both for encouragement and warning.

The Threat of Suffering

Hebrews was prepared for a specific local community. The writer knows his readers personally and identifies himself with them by using the personal pronouns "we" and "us." He expects soon to revisit them (13:19, 23). He mentions that they had become Christians in response to the preaching of disciples who had heard Jesus of Nazareth (2:3,4). He is alert to their failure to mature as teachers of the truth (5:11-14) and to their unselfish generosity in ministering to other Christians (6:9-11).

The statement "by this time you ought to be teachers " (5:12) implies that they had been believers for some time and were capable of engaging in a ministry, but they were not yet the most prominent members of the larger community; therefore the writer urged them to submit to their leaders (13:7, 17, 24).

The admonition, "Let us not give up meeting together, as some are in the habit of doing" (10:25) suggests that they were withdrawing from the main body of the church. They seem to have formed a small house-church. They had become weary with the constant struggle they faced as Christians (2:1-3; 3:13—4:2; 10:35-39; 12:12,13). They were showing signs of indifference and apathy (5:11-14; 6:9-12).

A common suggestion is that the group of Christians addressed in Hebrews were in Rome or in some community near Rome in southern Italy. In the closing paragraph the writer conveys the greetings of Italian Christians who are with him to the church at home (13:24). The most natural way of reading the text is that the writer was currently outside of Italy and that his sermon was prepared for a group of believers in or near Rome.

This proposal finds strong support in the reference to "earlier days," when the group had suffered public abuse, imprisonment, and confiscation of property: "Remember those earlier days after you had received the light, when you stood your ground in a great contest in the face of suffering. Sometimes you were publicly exposed to insult and persecution; at other times you stood side by side with those who were so treated. You sympathized with those in prison and joyfully accepted the confiscation of your property . . ." (10:32-34).

The description of the suffering endured is appropriate to the difficulties of the Jewish-Christians who were expelled from Rome by Claudius in A.D. 49.[9] Insult, persecution, and especially confiscation of property are normal under the conditions of a decree of expulsion. If this reading of Hebrews 10:32-34 is accurate, the writer prepared his sermon for some of the Jewish Christians who had been expelled from Rome with Aquila and Priscilla (Acts 18:1,2). They had endured exile, imprisonment, loss of property, and suffering, but not martyrdom (Heb. 12:4).

The situation now facing the community appears more serious than the earlier one. The statement that "in your struggle against sin you have *not yet* resisted to the point of shedding your blood" (12:4, italics added) suggests that martyrdom may become a fact of Christian experience in the near future. This sober statement climaxes a paragraph summarizing the experiences of men and women who are faithful to God under the circumstances of torture, flogging, chains, and execution (11:35—12:3). In the course of his sermon the writer twice warns the Christians against the unforgivable sin of holding Jesus Christ up to public contempt (6:4-6; 10:26-31). He urges his audience to fix their gaze upon Jesus, who "endured the cross, scorning its shame" so that they will not "grow weary and lose heart" (12:2,3). This establishes the context for the statement implying the possibility of martyrdom.

The evidence points in the direction of Rome in the period just before the outbreak of persecution under Nero. Immaturity and apathy were dangerous qualities to possess if there was the threat of arrest and death in the arena because you acknowledged you were a Christian. Ironically, the Jewish Christians for whom Hebrews was prepared had been involved in the evangelism of the Jewish community in Rome 15 years before. They had accepted the consequences of their bold faith and had stood their ground (10:32). Now they were older and tired; they had grown weary with the necessity of sustaining their commitment to Christ. When the threat of new persecution appeared imminent, they began considering withdrawal from the church (10:25) and perhaps from Christ.

The writer was a friend with a pastor's heart. He was concerned that if the Christians were arrested they might accept the Roman terms for their release— a public denial of Christ (6:6; 10:29). He remembered the conditions that Jesus had laid down for discipleship (Mark 8:34–38). He had warned that if anyone is ashamed of his association with Jesus and His words, even though his life is being threatened, Jesus will be ashamed of him when He comes as the final Judge (Mark 8:38). The writer's pastoral concern finds full expression in Hebrews. He wrote to encourage the believers in the face of this new crisis to stand firm in their faith and to warn them of their danger if they remained immature. They would incur the judgment of God if they failed to maintain their Christian position (Heb. 10:29-31,35-39).

His strongest encouragement was to remind his friends of the character of the Lord. He presents Jesus as their champion, who not only identifies Himself with them but who has released them from the fear of death (2:10-16). When standing before a Roman magistrate, Christians should fix their eyes on Jesus, the champion and "perfecter of our faith" (12:2). They will not enter the arena alone.

Jesus is also our great High Priest (2:17—3:1; 4:14—5:10; 6:19—8:2). Because He suffered He is able to strengthen those who are called to suffer (2:18). His own experience in being exposed to death enables Him to sympathize with human weakness (4:14,15). In a moving passage the writer reminds his friends that "during the days of Jesus' life on earth, he offered up prayers and petitions with loud cries and tears to the one who could have saved him from death, and he was heard because of his reverent submission" (5:7). The answer to His prayers and tears was not deliverance from death, but resurrection (13:20,21).

Jesus has become our great High Priest by virtue of His resurrection. The writer stresses that "he has become a high priest forever, in the order of Melchizedek" (6:20). The description of Jesus as a High Priest in the order of Melchizedek is the writer's way of presenting Jesus as a royal Priest who holds His office permanently because He was raised from the dead (7:1-3, 23,24). He is quick to add, "Therefore he is able to save completely those who come to God through him, because he always lives to intercede for them" (7:25). The exposition of the High Priesthood of Jesus establishes the point that the Lord cares for His people and will strengthen them. This was the message his friends needed to hear.

The Legacy of Stephen

The term *Hellenist* describes a Jewish Christian whose native language was Greek and who read his Bible in the Greek translation known as the Septuagint. Important Hellenists included Stephen and Philip and the men associated with them in their ministry in Jerusalem (Acts 6:1–6). The Hellenists provided the vision and the men for the expanding mission of the church which first resulted in the establishment of Gentile congregations (Acts 11:19-21). The man responsible for the book of Hebrews was a Hellenist, and he appears to owe some of his theology to the thinking of the early Hellenistic Christians. Some of the major emphases in Hebrews are developments of themes that appear in the speech of Stephen before the Sanhedrin in Jerusalem (Acts 7:2-53).

Stephen, for example, had referred to the pilgrim people of God who were called to leave familiar surround-

ings in obedience to the promise of God. He pointed to
Abraham who was called to be a wanderer, to Joseph who
was carried off to a foreign land, and to the Israelites who
became the pilgrim people of God after the exodus from
Egypt.

The theme of pilgrimage and promise is one of the
most distinctive notes in Hebrews. Israel in the wilderness
provides a familiar example of the experience of a people
who grew weary of a life based upon the promise of God.
They failed to gain entrance into God's promised rest
because of unbelief and disobedience (Heb. 3:7—4:11).
The reference to Israel's experience prepares for the presentation of the Christian life as a pilgrimage to the city of
God (11:8-16; 12:18-29; 13:13,14). The theme of pilgrimage becomes a useful means for calling the Christian
community to a life of faith and obedience in response to
the Word of God. The faith to which the writer points his
hearers is a confident reliance upon the promises of God
which have been confirmed through Jesus Christ. By
living their lives in accordance with the promises of God,
they will be able to make responsible decisions in the
present. It is this kind of faith which pilgrimage demands.

Another thought that Stephen developed is that there
is no necessary continuity between the people who receive the promises and those who finally enjoy their
fulfillment. What is required of the true people of God are
obedience and sustained faith in the promise of God.
Reviewing Israel's history, Stephen found it to be a record
of rebellion and resistance to the purposes of God which
reached its culmination in the betrayal and murder of
Jesus.

The writer of Hebrews also develops the consequences of Israel's history as a record of rebellion and
disobedience (3:7—4:11), but his emphasis is different
from that of Stephen. He wants his audience to recognize
that they are in danger of rejecting the voice of God, just

as Israel had done (3:7-12, 15; 4:1-3, 7, 11; 12:25). He repeatedly urges them to hold firmly to their confidence (3:1, 14; 4:14-16; 6:11,12; 10:19-25, 35-39). To fail to do so, to draw back from God and to sin deliberately after having received a knowledge of God's truth, is to invite the rejection and death which Israel experienced in the wilderness (10:26-31; 12:25).

The writer of Hebrews has drawn upon the legacy of Stephen, but he has enriched the theology and life of the Christian church by developing the insights he had received as a pastoral response to the sagging faith of his frightened Christian friends in Rome.

13
PRACTICAL
RIGHTEOUSNESS
James

James of Jerusalem

Although Jewish parents gave their son the name "Jacob," when he entered a world in which Greek was spoken everywhere he would be called "James." The man responsible for this letter was James, the brother of Jesus (Mark 6:3; Matt 13:55). James had not supported Jesus during His public ministry. In fact, none of Jesus' brothers believed in Him during that time (John 7:2-5). Their attitude toward Jesus may reflect the possibility that their mother Mary was at that time a widow. Responsibility for a widowed mother rested with the oldest son. When Jesus left Nazareth to begin His ministry He appeared to have shirked His responsibility. The care of Mary fell to James, the next oldest brother, and he may have resented this.

James's presence among the believers was due only to the fact that after the resurrection Jesus "appeared to

James" (1 Cor. 15:7). James's conversion accounts for the presence of Jesus' brothers with those who became the core of the Jerusalem church (Acts 1:13,14). When Peter was forced to flee from the city, responsibility for the leadership of the church was transferred to James (Acts 12:17; 15:13-21; 21:17-26; Gal. 1:19; 2:9, 12).

Under James, the church had remained loyal to the ritual law (Acts 21:20-26). As a result, the presentation of Jesus as the Messiah had been effective in bringing thousands of Jews to faith (Acts 21:20). But James's concern extended beyond Jerusalem to every center where Judaism could be found; his parish consisted of "all the Jews who live among the Gentiles" (Acts 21:21). He wrote his letter with the intention that it would circulate among the Jewish community in Palestine and throughout the world as an open letter to the "twelve tribes scattered among the nations" (Jas. 1:1).

Jews and Jewish-Christians

At the time when James wrote, Jewish-Christians were simply one group within Judaism. Apart from their conviction that Jesus of Nazareth was the Messiah promised by God, there was little to distinguish them from other Jews. They apparently worshiped side by side with their fellow Jews in the local synagogue. This is certainly the case presupposed by James when he takes up the matter of discrimination; he refers to the preferred treatment a man of wealth receives who "comes into your meeting" (2:2, synagogue in the Greek). The Jewish term "synagogue," rather than the Christian term "church," was appropriate for the communities addressed by James.

As the senior pastor of the Jerusalem church, it was necessary for James to keep in touch with Jewish-Christian leaders in other centers. He was aware that deep religious tensions had begun to surface between Jews and Jewish-Christians worshiping in the same synagogue. A different understanding of the Scriptures and of the significance of Jesus of Nazareth had begun to pull the two groups apart. It was all too easy for one group to call the other irresponsible. One of James's primary purposes in writing was to call attention to the seriousness of this situation before hostility—expressed in anger—caused irreparable harm: "My dear brothers, take note of this: Everyone should be quick to listen, slow to speak and slow to become angry, for man's anger does not bring about the righteous life that God desires" (1:19,20). James adds, "If anyone considers himself religious and yet does not keep a tight rein on his tongue, he deceives himself and his religion is worthless" (1:26).

The mention of the tongue anticipates the more extensive treatment of this theme in the body of the letter (3:1-12). Choosing sharp words that were designed to get his readers' attention, James describes the tongue as "a fire, a world of evil among the parts of the body" that can corrupt the whole person because it "is itself set on fire by hell" (3:6). The untamed tongue is "a restless evil, full of deadly poison" (3:8). James exposes the shame of the situation that those who gather in the synagogue for the blessing of God's name are capable of muttering a curse upon those whose view of the Messiah was different from their own: "With the tongue we praise our Lord and Father, and with it we curse men, who have been made in God's likeness. Out of the same mouth come praise and cursing. My brothers, this should not be" (3:9,10).

James denounces the bitter envy and selfish ambition which fosters such disorder, and calls for that godly wisdom which is peace-loving, impartial, and sincere (3:13-17). In the spirit of Jesus' beatitude, "Blessed are the peacemakers, for they will be called sons of God" (Matt. 5:9), James reminds *both* groups that "peacemakers who sow in peace raise a harvest of righteousness" (Jas. 3:18).

The fights and quarrels that had erupted could not be excused as expressions of excessive zeal. They called for earnest repentance (4:1-10). James's final word on this subject is addressed to both groups: "Brothers, do not slander one another. Anyone who speaks against his brother or judges him, speaks against the law and judges it. . . . But you—who are you to judge your neighbor?" (4:11,12).

Unfortunately, the counsel of James was ignored. The hostility between Jews and Jewish-Christians continued. Near the end of the century a new petition was added to the synagogue prayers asking God to curse the heretics and the Nazareans (the Jewish-Christians). That development effectively drove the Christians out of the synagogues. From that time forth the world was exposed to the sad spectacle of the church and the synagogue standing over against each other as two mutually exclusive and hostile camps.

Rich and Poor

James had another purpose in writing. It was necessary to denounce the oppression of the poor by the rich. James takes his place in the ranks of the prophets of Israel who had often found it necessary to expose the humiliation of the poor by those who possessed wealth and power. In his opening paragraphs James mentions "the brother in humble circumstances" and "the rich man" (1:9-11), but only the slightest hint is given of what is to follow.

In the body of the letter James reflects on Jesus' first beatitude, "Blessed are you who are poor, for yours is the kingdom of God" (Luke 6:20). He writes: "Listen, my dear brothers: Has not God chosen those who are poor in the eyes of the world to be rich in faith and to inherit the kingdom he promised those who love him? But you have insulted the poor. Is it not the rich who are exploiting you? Are they not the ones who are dragging you into court? Are they not the ones who are slandering the noble name of him to whom you belong?" (Jas. 2:5-7). What calls forth this searing judgment upon the Jewish-Christians in the synagogue is the favoritism shown toward a man of wealth while a poor man is dismissed as unimportant (2:1-7). James states in an unqualified way, "you have insulted the poor" (2:6)!

James reserved his sternest words, however, for the rich landowners who had defrauded those hired to work their estates (5:1-6). Such workmen depended upon the payment of the day's wage at the end of each day. The failure of the rich to honor the contractual agreement with their workers caused James to bristle with indignation. His words recall the preaching of Amos (Amos 2:6,7; 5:11-13, 16,17; 8:4-7), or of Jesus (Luke 6:20-26).

The oppressed poor are addressed as "brothers" (Jas. 1:9; 5:7, 9, 10, 12). Earlier in the letter James used this expression in its special Christian sense (2:1, "my brothers, as believers in our glorious Lord Jesus Christ . . ."). It is probable that this is his intention in this context as well. The poor, who were being humiliated by the rich, were primarily Jewish-Christians who worked on the estates of wealthy Jewish landholders. James's warning to the rich oppressors (5:1-6) is balanced by his counsel to the brothers to exercise patience and godly character, knowing that the Lord's coming is near (5:7-12). The sober reminder, "The Judge is standing at the door!" (5:9), provided comfort for the poor but terror for their oppressors. If the religious tensions which James had addressed were being aggravated by social and economic factors which pitted the rich against the poor, the need for James to encourage the oppressed Jewish-Christians in the life of faith was urgent.

Four Meditations

The letter of James is primarily ethical rather then theological in character. The issues it addresses are intensely practical: perseverance in the face of trials and testing (1:2-15), the character of true piety (1:27), the correlation between faith and deeds (2:14-26), the damage done by an uncontrolled tongue (3:2-12), among others. This concern for practical righteousness identifies the letter of James as an example of wisdom literature, much like the book of Proverbs in the Old Testament.

This observation is important for it prepares the reader to recognize that the distinctly Christian element in James does not consist in theological affirmations about Jesus. There is, for example, no mention of the cross or of Jesus' resurrection. The distinctly Christian element consists rather in the words or teaching of Jesus Himself as James had received them. Although Jesus' sayings are not actually quoted by James, his letter can be understood as a series of brief meditations expanding on one or more of the sayings of Jesus. The meditations cover *temptation* (1:2-18), the *law of love* (1:19—2:26), *evil speaking* (3:1—4:12), and *endurance* (4:13—5:20).

James begins with a meditation on one of the petitions of the Lord's Prayer, "Lead us not into temptation" (Matt. 6:13; Luke 11:4). He knew that Jesus was speaking about trial by suffering. Although the Christian is not spared from all exposure to "temptation" in this sense, God enables him to sustain the trials of life and to triumph over them. A believer's faith can be strengthened by the endurance of trials. Trials can produce the stability which encourages growth in wisdom, confidence in prayer, and maturity in Jesus Christ (Jas. 1:2-12).

The testing of faith, however, does not always lead to endurance and completeness in Christ. It can lead to sin. James takes up this fact of experience in the second half of his meditation on temptation (1:13-18). He insists that when temptation leads to sin it is not God's fault, but our own. The source of the problem is an "evil desire" in the human heart which drags a person away from God and entices him to sin. Sin, in turn, results in death (1:14,15). God is not the author of temptation (1:13). He is the holy and changeless One, who calls His people to experience life through the word of truth and provides them with every resource for overcoming temptation (1:17,18). Whenever temptation occurs it will lead the Christian either to defeat and captivity to sin, or to a stronger faith.

The subject of James's second meditation (1:9—2:26) is Jesus' summary of the law of love: "Love the Lord your God," and "Love your neighbor as yourself" (Matt. 22:37, 39). He actually quotes the second of the two commandments in James 2:8. But the mention of the Kingdom promised to those who love God in 2:5 shows that he has in mind both of the great commandments. The second meditation concerns the works of the law of love. James lends the full weight of his support to a practical piety; he calls for believers not merely to listen to the Word, but to do what the Word says (Jas. 1:22-25). His point of view is made clear when he identifies true piety as looking after orphans and widows (1:27), when he attacks the attitude that a person's worth is to be measured in terms of the wealth he possesses (2:1-9), and when he calls for the meeting of the physical needs of the poor and hungry (2:14-16). James insists that "faith by itself, if it is not accompanied by action, is dead" (2:17; see also v. 26). His Old Testament illustrations stress Abraham's love for God (2:20-24) and Rahab's love for her neighbor (2:25). Faith is shown to be genuine only by acts of love.

The synagogues torn by strife were scenes of evil speaking. James takes up this problem in the third meditation (3:1—4:12). Jesus had said, "What goes into the mouth does not defile a person; it is what comes out of his mouth that defiles him" (see Matt. 15:11). The mouth is the voice of the heart where "evil thoughts, murder, adultery, sexual immorality, theft, false testimony, slander" have been stored (Matt. 15:19). These poisons are released in evil-speaking.

James cautions anyone in the synagogue who desires to be a teacher that, as one who speaks with authority, the teacher is responsible for what he says (Jas. 3:1,2). Unfortunately, the tongue of man is often an untamed and destructive extension of an evil heart (3:3-8). Human speech can be notoriously fickle: "out of the same mouth come praise and cursing" (3:10). The tongue frequently expresses an earthly "wisdom" spawned by the devil which breeds "disorder and every evil practice" (3:15,16). If a man is truly wise and understanding, let him demonstrate this by integrity and by deeds done in humility (3:13, 17).

The quarrels which disrupted the synagogue community that was gathered for prayer indicated that there was no great distinction between the disciples of Moses and the disciples of Jesus. Both had attempted to approach God with unclean hands and impure hearts, and James calls both to repentance and humility (4:1-10). To speak evil against a brother or to judge him is to violate the royal law of love (4:11,12). Slander has no place in the life of those who know that the love of God must find its full expression in the love of neighbor.

James rounds out the series of meditations by returning to the theme of the first, the endurance of trials. The final meditation (4:13—5:20) relates the call to endurance to the return of the Lord (5:7). On the Mount of Olives, Jesus had instructed His disciples about this event, and said, "He who stands firm to the end will be saved" (Mark 13:13). James repeats this theme when he writes, "As you know, we consider blessed those who have [endured]" (5:11). He points to the prophets of the Old Testament and to Job as examples of those who remained faithful to God in the experience of suffering (5:11,12). The suffering

that James has in mind is primarily the social and economic oppression of the poor by wealthy landowners (5:1-
6). But he knows that suffering can come in the form of
trouble and sickness as well (5:13,14). In all of these
situations James calls for firm confidence in the compas-
sion and mercy of the Lord (5:11). Complaining (5:9) and
swearing (5:12) are inappropriate in the life of those who
know they will be vindicated by God. Faithful and fervent
prayer cultivates the quality of endurance which is to be
displayed in patient waiting for the return of the Lord
(5:7-11, 13-18).

In each of the four meditations James assumes that his
readers are already familiar with Jesus' teaching. The
manner in which he develops the implications of Jesus'
words for Christian living sets his letter apart among the
documents of the New Testament.

14
ASSAULT UPON THE CHURCH
First and Second Peter; Jude

First Peter—the New Israel of God

When Herod Agrippa I arrested Peter with the intention of putting him to death, Peter was released from prison by an act of God (Acts 12:1-19). Leaving Jerusalem in the night, he fled northward to Antioch, far out of Agrippa's reach (Gal. 2:11). Although he slipped back into Jerusalem for the council convened over the question whether Gentiles had to be circumcised (Acts 15:6-14), his life could have been endangered if he had remained. He must have left soon afterward and apparently turned northward into Syria and then westward through Roman Asia, Macedonia, and Achaia. He certainly passed through Corinth, where he attracted a strong following (1 Cor. 1:12, "One of you says, . . . 'I follow Cephas' ''; see also 3:21,22; 9:5). His final destination, however, was Rome, where he took up residence.

Peter was in Rome during the troubled months im-

mediately following the great fire which nearly destroyed
the city. He anticipated that the government would have
to shift the blame for the fire to some group and that this
could mean trouble for the Christians. They were already
an object of popular resentment because their behavior
differed radically from a pagan life-style. He knew that if
persecution broke out in Rome, it could set off a chain
reaction which would affect Christians in the provinces as
well. Peter's first letter was written to warn Christians
scattered throughout Roman Asia of this possibility.

God had given Peter the special task of preaching the
gospel to the Jews (Gal. 2:7). When he addresses his letter
to "God's elect, strangers in the world, scattered throughout Pontus, Galatia, Cappadocia, Asia and Bithynia"
(1 Pet. 1:1), it is natural to think of Greek-speaking
Jewish-Christians for whom Peter assumed responsibility
because he was the apostle to the Jews. This proves not to
be true, however. Peter is actually writing to Gentiles who
have become Christians and who have inherited the titles
and privileges of ancient Israel. He writes: "But you are a
chosen people, a royal priesthood, a holy nation, a people
belonging to God, that you may declare the praises of him
who called you out of darkness into his wonderful light.
Once you were not a people, but now you are the people of
God; once you had not received mercy, but now you have
received mercy" (2:9,10).

It is Gentiles who were called out of darkness into
God's light (Isa. 9:2; 42:6,7; 49:6), those who were
formerly not God's people but who have become God's
people as the result of the extension of God's mercy. By
using the language of the Old Testament (Exod. 19:5,6;
Hos. 2:23), Peter gives to the Gentile churches a sense of
their identity and continuity with the ancient people of
God.

That his readers are primarily Gentiles is confirmed
when Peter refers to their pagan past and to the response of

their peers to their conversion: "For you have spent enough time in the past doing what pagans choose to do—living in debauchery, lust, drunkenness, orgies, carousing and detestable idolatry. They think it strange that you do not plunge with them into the same flood of dissipation, and they heap abuse on you" (1 Pet. 4:3,4).

Although Peter had been given a special commission to preach to Jews, his pastoral ministry was to Gentiles as well who had become the new Israel of God.

Faith Refined by Fire

In response to the developing crisis in Rome, Peter warns the Christians of Roman Asia that they "may have to suffer [grief in] various trials" (1:6, *RSV*). But he is quick to point out that the experience of trials has a positive value: "These have come so that your faith . . . may be proved genuine and may result in praise, glory and honor when Jesus Christ is revealed" (1:7). The Christian's "pledge of good faith" to Jesus Christ is tested in daily life, and especially in the crisis of persecution. Although a believer is never exempt from the refiner's fire, the character of true faith is displayed in the ordeal.

In order to prepare his readers for the trial of their faith Peter develops the important consideration that they may be called to stand before a Roman magistrate. In that situation they must look beyond the judgment of men to the judgment seat of God before whom all men will stand. This double perspective of standing before men and before God is the key to much of the letter.

It is before men that grief may be suffered, but faith that proves genuine will be vindicated when Jesus Christ is revealed as the final Judge (1:6,7). In court, pagans may accuse the believers of doing wrong, but they will ultimately "see your good deeds and glorify God on the day he visits us" for judgment (2:12). Christians may be misrepresented maliciously in a Roman court of law, but those who have slandered them will be made ashamed when they stand before God (3:13-16). Although pagans use their courts to heap abuse upon Christians, "they will give account to him who is ready to judge the living and the dead" (4:5, *RSV*). Consequently, Christians can remain steadfast in their faith and unashamed when condemned unjustly. They will be vindicated, even if it must be at the judgment throne of God.

In the course of the letter there is an important shift in perspective. The prospect of suffering that was set before the readers as a remote possibility (1:6,7, "you may have to suffer various trials," *RSV*), has been confirmed by 4:12 ("Dear friends, do not be surprised at the painful trial you are suffering, as though something strange were happening to you"). Suddenly suffering as a Christian was no longer a remote possibility. It was a matter of present and certain expectation (4:12-16). In the light of this shift, it may be proper to regard 1:1—4:11 as the limits of the letter Peter was in the process of writing; 4:12—5:14 represents a hastily written postscript added when persecution broke out.

Peter's response to the efforts of Rome to destroy the Christian movement puts persecution in its proper setting. Trials are not to be an occasion for surprise; they signify participation in the sufferings of Christ, and are the prelude to vindication (4:12,13). The intensity of the conflict between the church and a hostile world indicates that the time of judgment is near. The appropriate response is an open display of the integrity of Christian commitment (4:16-19).

Although anxiety is normal when life is threatened, the source of Christian courage is the firm conviction that God cares for His people (5:6,7). Peter calls his readers to recognize the demonic character of the persecution launched by the government. The order for Christians to be arrested and put to death came from Nero, but its ultimate source was the enemy of God's people, the devil, who "prowls around like a roaring lion looking for some-one to devour" (5:8). Christians are to resist him by standing firm in the faith. Churches separated by distance find a bond of brotherhood encouraged through the common experience of suffering (5:9). The sufferings of a martyr church have meaning because God cares and restores those who draw their strength from Him (5:10,11).

Peter closes his letter by conveying the greetings of the church in Rome (5:13). He designates the imperial city by the code word "Babylon," where the new Israel of God found itself captive. His letter conveys a vivid impression of what it means to live as a Christian in a hostile environment where holiness of life must be displayed through the conduct of daily affairs and in the routine relationships of life.

Second Peter; Jude: Attack on False Teaching

The life of the church could be disrupted as seriously by the presence of false teaching as by persecution. Teachers who rejected the authority of the apostolic tradition and who substituted their own convictions for those received by the churches could radically alter the character of a congregation. What was at stake was the integrity of Christian conviction and behavior. Second Peter and Jude address the threat posed by the presence of false prophets and teachers who had won a following in the churches.

The false teaching they attack was the libertine attitude that morality is a matter of personal choice. A reckless disregard for the law of God encouraged a situational morality, the persuasion that what was appropriate behavior could be determined only by the situation. What was actually involved was an unwillingness to exercise self-discipline in personal relationships. With one voice, Peter and Jude condemn the arrogance of the false teachers and the folly of those who have listened to them.

The false teachers traveled as missionaries from one church center to another and apparently secured their support from the offerings they received. Peter exposes their lack of integrity: "In their greed these teachers will exploit you with stories they have made up" (2 Pet. 2:3). He describes them as "experts in greed" (2:14), who love "wages of wickedness" (2:15). Jude denounces them as "shepherds who feed only themselves" (Jude 12), who "boast about themselves and flatter others for their own advantage" (Jude 16).

The theme of the false teachers' preaching was sexual freedom. With indignation Peter writes, "They mouth empty, boastful words and, by appealing to the lustful desires of sinful human nature, they entice people who are just escaping from those who live in error. They promise them freedom, while they themselves are slaves of depravity—for a man is a slave to whatever has mastered him" (2 Pet. 2:18,19).

Jude was also filled with indignation. He describes the false teachers as "godless men, who change the grace of our God into a license for immorality and deny Jesus Christ our only Sovereign and Lord" (Jude 4). Yet these men did not hesitate to share in the meal at which the Lord's Supper was celebrated. Jude exclaims: "These men are blemishes at your love feasts, eating with you without the slightest qualm" (Jude 12). Peter and Jude agree that the actions of the false teachers exposed them to severe judgment.

The theme of judgment which runs through both letters provides an important clue to the relationship between 2 Peter and Jude. The two letters share much in common. The correspondence between 2 Peter 2:1—3:3 and Jude 4-18 can be shown in a table:

2 Peter	2:1-3,	4,		6,		10,	11,	12,	15,	13-17,	18;	3:1-3
Jude		4,	6,	7,	8,	9,	10,	11,	12,13,		16,	17,18	

These sections are precisely where the exposure of the false teachers is concentrated. They consist of examples, drawn primarily from the Old Testament, of God's judgment on rebellion and false teaching. The correspondence between 2 Peter and Jude extends to content and to the order in which the examples are taken up. The actual expression of each writer, however, is distinctive. This fact precludes the simple judgment that one borrowed from the other but points in another direction. Both writers drew independently upon a common source, a collection of Old Testament texts documenting that rebellion and false teaching incur divine punishment. Peter may have been responsible for putting the collection together. Such collections were valuable aids to church leaders in their fight against those who encouraged a disregard of the moral dimension in Christian commitment.

Jude, who identifies himself only as "a servant of Jesus Christ and a brother of James" (Jude 1), is actually a younger brother of Jesus (Mark 6:3). He had come to faith as a result of the resurrection-appearance to James (1 Cor. 15:7; Acts 1:14), and eventually took his own place among the leaders of the church, with responsibility for a number of congregations.

Jude was prepared to write about Christian salvation, but he felt compelled to write the present letter (Jude 3). What caused him to alter his purpose was a developing crisis in his churches. Congregations were being divided over the practical issue of what constituted Christian freedom (v. 19). Recognizing the seriousness of the situation, Jude sounds a battle cry, calling all Christians to a defense of the apostolic faith and to holiness of life (vv. 3,4). He drew freely upon the apostolic tradition to expose the danger of judgment which those who rebel against God risk by their actions (vv. 5-16). The arrival of the false teachers confirmed the accuracy of the apostolic warning that "in the last times there will be scoffers who will follow their own ungodly desires" (vv. 17,18). The presence of error and division is an incentive to growth in faith and prayer (vv. 20,21). Jude urges his communities to engage in an active mission to persuade the lawless to submit to the apostolic rule of faith and practice (vv. 22,23).

The occasion for Peter's second letter (2 Pet. 3:1) was different. The apostle knew that he would soon die. He determined to leave his churches a record of matters that were especially important to him which would provide access to his thought after his death (1:12-15). In 2 Peter the church possesses the apostle's memoirs (1:16-18).

Jude's intention to write about the salvation which Christians share was actually carried out by Peter in the opening segment of his letter (2 Pet. 1:3-11). He urges the believers to demonstrate the call of God upon their lives by cultivating the qualities of Christian life which exhibit Jesus Christ to the world (1:5-8). The Christian who seeks to mature in faith and knowledge is assured that God "has given us everything we need for life and godliness" (1:3). His resources include the witness of those who were with Jesus (1:16-18) and the authority of the prophetic Scriptures (1:19-21).

These were important considerations because of the current situation in the churches, marked by moral confusion and rebellion. Although the apostles had not followed "cleverly invented stories" when they proclaimed the power and coming of the Lord (1:16), false teachers did not hesitate to bolster their authority with "stories they have made up" (2:3). Peter exposes the folly of "those who follow the corrupt desire of the sinful nature and despise authority" (2:10). But he also found it necessary to address a related issue about which Jude had said nothing. Those who rejected the binding authority of God's moral law now scoffed at the teaching of the church concerning the Lord's return (3:3,4). The delay encouraged them to believe that there was no urgency for moral righteousness.

Peter corrects their error (3:5-7) and calls the churches to recognize God's gracious purpose in the delay (3:9). God's patience expresses His desire for the repentance of sinners (3:15). Nevertheless, there is a limit to the divine patience. The day of the Lord will come and the world will be destroyed by fire (3:7,10,12). Only believers who conduct themselves in the light of that awesome reality will find that God has prepared for them "a new heaven and a new earth, the home of righteousness" (3:13).

15
THE TESTS OF CHRISTIAN LIFE AND FELLOWSHIP
First, Second and Third John

First John—Life in God

When John prepared his Gospel the church in Asia was engaged in a fierce struggle. A new breed of teachers had made their appearance who attempted to work out a compromise with paganism by interpreting Christian faith as a form of philosophy. They openly challenged the teaching commonly received in the churches. They denied, for example, that Jesus of Nazareth was the Son of God who had come in the flesh. John, the last surviving apostle, had prepared his Gospel in response to them. He appears to have written 1 John as an introduction to the Gospel.

Although it is common to regard 1 John as a letter, it has few of the characteristics of a normal letter. The opening lines do not identify the writer or those whom he addressed. No prayer is expressed at the beginning, and there is no word of greeting or farewell at the end. These are the elements in John's two shorter communications which clearly identify them as letters (2 John 1-3,13; 3 John 1,2,15).

The popular opinion that 1 John is a typical letter is based upon the frequency with which John speaks about writing to his people (1:4; 2:1,7,8,12-14,26; 5:13). The designation of the readers as "dear children" (2:1,12,13,18,28; 3:7; 4:4; 5:21) or as "dear friends" (2:7; 3:21; 4:1,7) conveys an impression of intimacy common in personal letters. But the document which accompanied the Gospel does not have the form of a letter. It appears to be a written sermon through which John sought to address his readers with the directness he would have used if he could have spoken with them face to face. The pastoral concern and affection evident in 1 John was appropriate in a sermon.

Although John used much of the same vocabulary and expression found in the Gospel, his sermon addressed more directly than the Gospel the spiritual and pastoral problems of the hour. For example, it responds to the activity of the false teachers in a manner that would have been inappropriate in the Gospel. The Gospel of John deals with the time of Jesus; 1 John is concerned with the apostle's own time about A.D. 90, as the first century began to draw to a close.

The sermon develops one of the major emphases of the Gospel, the theme of "life in God." John summarizes his message for his readers when he writes, "We proclaim to you what we have seen and heard, so that you also may have fellowship with us. And our fellowship is with the Father and with his Son, Jesus Christ" (1:3). The "fellowship" about which John speaks is an expression of the life which the Christian enjoys with God as a result of Jesus' death and resurrection. A major theme in John's Gospel is that in His resurrection Jesus returns to the Father. But He also returns to His disciples in order to unite them in Himself with the Father. This reality can be understood as the sharing of a common life. John now emphasizes for his audience that this common life is shared both with the Father and with the Son.

John's readers had not participated in the events announced in the Gospel. His purpose is to share with them what the eyewitnesses of Jesus' life and deeds experienced. From the beginning they had heard and seen and even touched Jesus (1:1). John may have been thinking especially of that Sunday evening a week after Easter when Thomas had been invited to touch the wounds of the risen Lord (John 20:24-29). His sermon was intended to extend this sense of sharing in the reality of the Resurrection to all Christians everywhere. John's ministry was to those upon whom Jesus had pronounced the blessing, "Blessed are those who have not seen and yet have believed" (John 20:29).

These considerations indicate that the thread of thought in 1 John will run closely parallel to the development in the Gospel. The special value of the sermon is that John sets forth several practical tests for recognizing the presence of life in God; possession of the divine life will be demonstrated at the level of personal conduct. John expects a close correlation between the creed a Christian recites and the actions he performs. He continually reminds the believers who they are, in order to reinforce his description of what they do. Christians are, for example, "in God" or "in the light"; they have fellowship with God and with one another; they "abide in him"; they are "of God"; they "know God" and "have eternal life." As a result, they love God and one another; they "keep the commandments"; they "walk in the light"; they confess that Jesus Christ came in the flesh.

Many of John's statements are put together in such a way as to show that these two aspects of Christian experience cannot be separated. What Christians *do* demonstrates who Christians *are*. A few examples from 1 John indicate John's approach:

What a Christian does	*What a Christian is*
2:10 "Whoever loves his brother	lives in the light."
2:29 "Everyone who does what is right	has been born of him."
3:24 "Those who obey his commands	live in him, and he in them."
4:15 "If anyone acknowledges that Jesus is the Son of God	God lives in him and he in God."

John uses this same device to describe those who are not Christians:

What an unbeliever does	*What an unbeliever is*
3:8 "He who does what is sinful	is of the devil."
3:14 "Anyone who does not love	remains in death."
3:15 "Anyone who hates his brother	is a murderer."
4:3 "Every spirit that does not acknowledge Jesus	is not from God."

John defends obedience, love, and faith as the essential marks of life in God. He organizes his thought around three statements of faith:

1. "God is light; in him there is no darkness at all" (1:5).
2. "This is the last hour" (2:18).
3. "Jesus Christ has come in the flesh" (4:2).

Each of these statements expresses in its own way the good news declared in John's Gospel that God has acted decisively to redeem His people through His Son Jesus. Taken together they are "the Word of life" which was "from the beginning" which John proclaims to his readers (1:1). Each of the statements introduces a new unit of thought in which John applies the tests of obedience and love to Christian experience. In the course of the sermon he writes about walking in the light (1:5—2:17), living for the future (2:18—3:24), and believing the truth (4:1—5:21).

The statement that "God is light; in him there is no darkness at all" (1:5) prepares for the related statement that "the darkness is passing and the true light is already shining" (2:8). The contrast between light and darkness is taken from the prologue to John's Gospel (John 1:1-18). There the apostle speaks of the coming of the light into the darkness of the world (John 1:5,9). John's point in 1 John 1:5 is that we know the character of God precisely because of the dawning of the light in history in the ministry of Jesus Christ. His presence in the world explains why the darkness is passing.

The Christian confession that "God is light," however, must be validated by Christian behavior: "If we claim to have fellowship with him yet walk in darkness, we lie and do not [put the truth into practice]" (1:6). John therefore applies the test of obedience to Christian experience (1:6—2:6). A series of conditional sentences develops the moral implications of fellowship in the light and sharply defines the issue of obedience (1:6-10). The assurance that sins are forgiven because Jesus speaks to the Father in defense of Christians, issues from obedience to the commands of Christ (2:1-6). The Christian "must walk as Jesus did" (2:6).

John also applies to Christian confession the test of love (2:7-17). The matter of obeying the commands of Jesus (2:3) becomes intensely practical when John calls attention to one commandment which is both old and new (2:7,8). It is old because God gave the law of love to His people long ago (Lev. 19:18). It is new because it was taken up by Jesus and given a new content with the love He demonstrated for His disciples. The commandment John has in mind is the "new" commandment Jesus gave His disciples to love one another (John 13:34). Love for a brother is thus the test of Christian life (1 John 2:9-11) and serves to identify those whose "sins have been forgiven" and who "have known the Father" (2:12,13).

The warnings in 2:15-17 serve as a bridge to the second unit of thought. The declaration that the world is passing away (2:17) repeats the good news that "the darkness is passing and the true light is already shining" (2:8). It also anticipates the announcement which introduces the next unit, "Dear children, this is the last hour" (2:18).

The key note of the first unit was light; the dominant note of the second unit is life. John writes: "And this is what he promised us—even eternal life" (2:25). In the Gospel, John stressed that Jesus made eternal life the present possession of those who believe His word. This understanding is presupposed in the sermon as well. The emphasis falls upon those who enjoy life because they have been born of God (2:29) and are the children of God (3:1,2).

In the second unit John develops the statement of faith in the light of false teaching among the churches (2:18—3:3); he then points out the practical implications of the statement in terms of obedience (3:4-10) and love (3:11-

17). The unit is rounded off with words of assurance (3:18-24).

The conviction that "this is the last hour" found strong support in the disturbing situation John describes. Jesus had taught that His final appearing would be preceded by times of trouble and stress. False teachers would seek to lead His chosen people astray (Mark 13:21-23). John recognized these conditions in his own day. He boldly applies the designation "antichrists" to a group of teachers who only recently had infiltrated the churches and had disrupted their peace (1 John 2:18). They had sinned against the truth by denying that Jesus is the Christ (2:21,22). They had been guilty of murder in their hatred of the brothers (3:14,15). They had now left, taking a sizable group with them (2:19). John addresses those who remained, and reminds them of the tests of obedience and love which separate those who have received life from God from those who are not His children but belong to the devil (3:7-10).

The key note of the final unit (4:1—5:21) is faith. Those who claim to know God and to be born of God must demonstrate their integrity in their confession of faith. John reduces the church's confession to the single point that "Jesus Christ has come in the flesh" (4:2). The importance of the creed is kept before the readers as John confesses his own faith:

- "God sent his one and only Son into the world" (4:9).
- "The Father has sent his Son to be the Savior of the world" (4:14).
- "Jesus is the Son of God" (4:15; 5:5).
- "Jesus is the Christ" (5:1).
- "The Son of God has come" (5:20).

This is what every Christian must confess and believe.

John develops this conviction as he had done in the first two units. After setting forth the statement of faith in 4:1-6, he applies the tests of love (4:7-12) and obedience

(5:3-21) to those who claim to be believers. Each of the sections concludes on the note of assurance and confidence in God (4:16-18; 5:13-21). At the close of the sermon John restates the theme of life in God: "We are in him who is true—even in his Son Jesus Christ. He is the true God and eternal life" (5:20).

Second John—Concern for Love and Truth

John's second letter was addressed to one of the Asian churches. "The chosen lady and her children" (v. 1) is John's way of referring to the church and its individual members, while "the children of your chosen sister" (v. 13) are persons in John's own church. The apostle could write briefly because he hoped to visit them in the near future. He had much to share, but preferred to speak with people directly (v. 12). The purpose of his letter was to alert the church that he was coming. The statement that "it has given me joy to find some of your children [living by] the truth" (v. 4) implies that some others had departed from the truth.

Second John appears to be a summary of 1 John. Almost all of the content corresponds to the fuller treatment found in the sermon which accompanied John's Gospel. The tests of love and obedience, for example, are expressed concisely in verses 5,6. The life of love is precisely the life of obedience to the commandments of the Lord and is displayed in love one for another.

The remainder of the body of the letter is devoted to the matter of true and false teaching, and focuses upon the Incarnation (vv. 7-11). The situation is clearly parallel to 1 John where the apostle warned that "many false prophets have gone out into the world" (1 John 4:1). Here in 2 John he states that "many deceivers . . . have gone out into the world" (v. 7). The test of true doctrine is the confession that Jesus Christ has come in the flesh. The acknowledgment that Jesus of Nazareth was the incarnate

Son of God provided a simple indicator for discerning whether strangers who claimed to be authorized teachers of the church were actually committed to the truth.

John cautions the believers not to lend any encouragement to a teacher who has deviated from the truth (vv. 10,11). The refusal of hospitality and greeting to a teacher who denies the truth is not a violation of Christian love but the determination to resist the spread of false teaching. What someone believes and teaches about Jesus Christ is of ultimate importance because it concerns "the truth, which lives in us and will be with us forever" (v. 2).

Third John—Living According to the Truth

John's third letter is a brief personal note to Gaius, a close friend. Its tone is friendly and intimate. The letter responds to qualities in Gaius which had already won the apostle's respect and affection (vv. 3,4). Gaius had distinguished himself by opening his home to strangers traveling in the service of the churches (vv. 5-8). Such men depended upon a network of homes where they could receive shelter for the night and fresh provisions for the next day of travel. Tangible expressions of Christian love found in the home of Gaius had eased the hardships of travel for many missionaries (vv. 3,4,6). John remembered Jesus' instruction when He had washed the disciples' feet: "I tell you the truth, whoever accepts anyone I send accepts me; and whoever accepts me accepts the one who sent me" (John 13:20). The faithfulness displayed by Gaius in extending hospitality to the true messengers of God demonstrated that he was living according to the truth (3 John 6-8).

The obedience and love of Gaius was thrown into bold relief by John's experience with Diotrephes, an elder who was abusing his authority. He had openly opposed John and sought to undermine him by malicious gossip (vv. 9,10). His contempt for John was matched by his response to the emissaries of the church: "He refuses to welcome the brothers. He also stops those who want to do so and puts them out of the church" (v. 10). Diotrephes's sense of self-importance, his calloused attitude toward John, and his reckless action in expelling from the church those who sought to demonstrate love, condemn him as one who "has not seen God" (v. 11).

Demetrius, on the other hand, "is well spoken of by everyone—and even by the truth itself" (v. 12). Although this man is otherwise unknown, he must have been a mutual friend to John and Gaius who continued to deserve the apostle's commendation. When John comes he will confer with Gaius (vv. 13,14), but he will call the church to discipline Diotrephes for failing to live according to the truth (v. 10).

The power struggle implied by 3 John must have been painful to the apostle, but he found himself comforted by Jesus' declaration, "You are my friends if you do what I command. I no longer call you servants. . . . Instead, I have called you friends" (John 15:14,15). John takes up the designation "friends" and applies it to the believers who have passed the practical tests of Christian life, obedience, love, and faith: "Peace to you. The friends here send their greetings. Greet the friends there by name" (3 John 15).

16
THE TRIUMPH OF GOD
Revelation

Conflict with Rome

When John prepared his Gospel (A.D. 90) he was the senior pastor of the church in Ephesus, with responsibility for the supervision of six other churches in Roman Asia as well. The last surviving member of the disciples whom Jesus had chosen had reached an advanced age. His major concern was to strengthen the churches of Asia torn by false teaching (1 John; 2 John) and by struggles for power (3 John). He was still alive five years later when a new crisis threatened the existence of the church in Asia.

Occupying the imperial throne was Domitian (A.D. 81-96), who had encouraged the worship of the emperor as divine. The pageantry of the Roman spectacles may have encouraged some people to speak of the emperors as if they were gods, but Domitian's predecessors certainly knew that this was not true. Augustus and Claudius were content to wait until their death before the Roman Senate declared they had been deified. But Domitian was impatient and was prepared to be recognized as a god in his own lifetime. He may have attempted to enforce some kind of emperor worship. He is remembered as the first Roman emperor to insist on being addressed as "our lord and our god."[10]

Some of the cities in the province of Asia accepted the new cult of Rome and the emperor enthusiastically. In Pergamum there was an Augusteum, a temple devoted to "the divine Augustus," where the image of the emperor was venerated and those who embraced the imperial cult could worship. Ephesus petitioned for permission to build an Augusteum of its own. These developments encouraged conflict between the church and the empire. Refusal to bow before the Augusteum or the image of the emperor could be understood as disloyalty to Rome. Christians could not acknowledge Domitian as "our lord and our god" because these divine titles belong to Jesus alone (John 20:28).

Toward the end of Domitian's reign, persecution of the Christians broke out in the province of Asia. John was arrested and was sent into political exile to the Mediterranean island of Patmos (Rev. 1:9). In Pergamum, one of the local Christians, Antipas, was put to death (2:13). The situation of the Christians in Smyrna (2:10) and Philadelphia (3:10) became precarious. The course of events suggested that the Christians in Asia must prepare for a life and death struggle with Rome.

In these circumstances John wrote to the seven mainland churches he had served and loved and related to them the series of visions he had received while worshiping on the Lord's Day (Rev. 1:10). By introducing his book as "the revelation of Jesus Christ" (1:1) John indicates that Jesus is the actual author of what he has written. His own role was simply to record what he had seen: "Write on a scroll what you see and send it to the seven churches: to Ephesus, Smyrna, Pergamum, Thyatira, Sardis, Philadelphia and Laodicea" (1:11). Those who listen to the message of this book can expect to hear the voice of Jesus (1:17-19).

The primary theme of Revelation is the coming of God's kingdom. The message of the book is that the triumph of God's rule will be celebrated in history. In a vision of the heavenly court, for example, John hears the sound of a trumpet and a chorus of loud voices that declared: "The kingdom of the world has become the kingdom of our Lord and of his Christ, and he will reign for ever and ever" (11:15). In response to this announcement, a hymn of worship celebrates that God has taken His great power and has begun to reign (11:16-18). The later chapters in Revelation tell in detail how Jesus comes to be enthroned as "the Lord of lords and King of kings" (17:14; see also 19:16), and provide the assurance that "with him will be his called, chosen and faithful followers" (17:14). This was the assurance that the oppressed Christians in Asia needed to receive. Although the officials of the imperial cult may have the ability to humiliate them now, the triumph of God will take place in history, and they will participate in the victory celebration.

The Work of Prophecy

Revelation claims to be a work of prophecy (1:3; 22.7,10,18,19). It is an authoritative word of assurance and judgment issued by God and delivered by the exalted Lord (1:1). John identifies the source of his message as "the word of God and the testimony of Jesus Christ" (1:2). "The word of God" is, of course, the most familiar element in prophecy; the task of the prophet is to declare the word of the Lord. "The testimony of Jesus Christ" is something new. It is the form that prophecy takes now that Jesus has come. In a later vision John is told by an angel that "the testimony of Jesus is the spirit of prophe-

cy" (19:10). Jesus Christ, risen from the dead and exalted
as Lord, is the source of Christian prophecy (1:12-20).
Because Revelation is a prophecy, the One who really
speaks is Jesus Christ.

The scope of the prophecy extends to the present and
the future. John received the instruction, "Write, therefore, what you have seen, what is now and what will take
place later" (1:19). What John has "seen" describes the
entire book, which was conveyed in a series of visions.
But the distinction between "what is now" and "what will
take place later" provides an important key to the structure
of the book. A review of the current situation of the
churches (chaps. 1—3) serves as a prelude to a disclosure
of what will yet occur (chaps. 4—22).

Like Isaiah (Isa. 6:1-13) or Ezekiel (Ezek. 1:1—2:2)
in the Old Testament, John was set apart for his prophetic
ministry by a vision of the glorified Lord (Rev. 1:12-20).

*John's vision identified Jesus as the Lord of the
church.* John sees Him standing among the seven golden
lampstands, symbolic of the seven churches of Asia
Minor (1:13,20). The details of the vision are repeated in
chapters 2 and 3 to identify the exalted Christ as the
speaker in the seven letters (2:1,8,12,18; 3:1,7,14).
Although the conditions in each church vary, all the
letters have five features in common:

1. The Lord identifies himself ("These are the words of
   him who . . .").
2. He reviews the situation of the church in the world ("I
   know . . .").
3. He instructs the church ("Remember . . . repent . . .
   be faithful . . .").
4. He gives a promise to the faithful Christian ("To him
   who overcomes . . .").
5. He appeals for obedience ("He who has an ear, let him
   hear. . .)."

In the exercise of His Lordship, Jesus offers assurance

and encouragement to faithful believers but rebuke and stern warning to those who have been spiritually careless. The letters indicate that the churches were facing danger not only from a hostile Roman society (2:10,13; 3:10) but from segments of the Jewish population who were bringing slanderous accusations against the Christians (2:9; 3:9,10). They also disclose that the churches were threatened from within. The tolerance of false teaching and coldness of heart expose Christians to the discipline of divine judgment (2:4,5,14-16,20-23; 3:1,2,15-19). Only the churches of Smyrna and Philadelphia receive the unqualified approval of the Lord. The repetition of the solemn call to hear what the Spirit is saying to the churches (plural!) is a sober reminder that what is said to each church is said to them all.

Not only is Jesus the Lord of the church, the message of the prophecy in chapters 4—22 is that He is also the Lord of history. In a dramatic vision the prophet enters the heavenly throne room where his attention is fixed upon a sealed scroll which no one could open (5:1-4). When John began to weep, a member of the heavenly court comforted him: " 'Do not weep! See, the Lion of the tribe of Judah, the Root of David, has triumphed. He is able to open the scroll and its seven seals.' Then I saw a Lamb, looking as if it had been slain, standing in the center of the throne, encircled by the four living creatures and the elders" (5:5,6). Jesus the Messiah can break the seven seals on the basis of His conquest of death in the Resurrection.

As each seal is broken, the prophet is shown a brief scene unfolding the course of world history:

- First Seal: Christ's victory in His first coming (6:1,2)
- Second Seal: War (6:3,4)
- Third Seal: Famine (6:5,6)
- Fourth Seal: Pestilence (6:7,8)
- Fifth Seal: The experience of the martyrs (6:9-11)
- Sixth Seal: The catastrophes that immediately precede

the return of the Lord (6:12-17)
• Seventh Seal: "Silence in heaven" (8:1)

The seven seals disclose the events which must take place before God's Kingdom can be revealed. They are a pictorial representation of Jesus' teaching concerning the necessary signs of the approaching end of the age: "When you hear of wars and rumors of wars, do not be alarmed. Such things must happen, but the end is still to come. Nation will rise against nation, and kingdom against kingdom. There will be earthquakes in various places, and famines. These are the beginning of birth pains" (Mark 13:7,8). The first five seals are as characteristic of our own age as they were of John's.

The presentation of Christ as the One who is worthy to open the seals demonstrates that He is the Lord of world history. When Christians experience suffering in the world, God is not taken by surprise. These hardships are simply the events which must take place before the disclosure of the final triumph of God.

The content of the seventh seal is, of course, surprising. The breaking of the final seal should permit the scroll to be unrolled and its message proclaimed. Not until much later in the prophecy is the silence of the seventh seal (8:1) broken by God's triumphant Word (19:11-13). Between these two points the shape of God's future is unveiled as the reader is taken over the ground covered by the vision of the seals again and again. The blowing of the seven trumpets (chaps. 8—11) and the pouring out of the seven bowls of wrath (chaps 15; 16) express the certainty of God's coming judgment and assure the oppressed people of God that He will deliver them from their persecutors.

The scroll proves to be Jesus' last will and testament. The will became valid with His death. But with His resurrection (1:18), He became the executor of the will who will see that its provisions are enforced. In the ancient world, as today, a will consisted of two parts—a description of the inheritance and a list of the heirs. This is precisely the character of the Lamb's scroll in chapter 5. It is identified in later visions as the Lamb's scroll (book) of life (13:8; 21:27) or simply the scroll (book) of life (17:8; 20:12). The description of the inheritance of the saints was already suggested in the promises extended to faithful believers in the letters to the seven churches. In the final vision John discovers that the inheritance is the enjoyment of God forever: "And I heard a loud voice from the throne saying, 'Now the dwelling of God is with men, and he will live with them. They will be his people, and God himself will be with them and be their God. He will wipe every tear from their eyes. There will be no more death or mourning or crying or pain, for the old order of things has passed away.'

"He who was seated on the throne said, 'I am making everything new!' Then he said, 'Write this down, for these words are trustworthy and true' " (21:3-5).

God's covenant people will then exchange a life sustained by the promises of God for the fulfillment of every promise in the immediate presence of God.

The writing on the front and back side of the scroll (5:1) covers the list of the heirs. Included are the names of all those who have confessed the name of Jesus and who have been faithful to Him, often at the cost of their lives (6:9; 20:4). The disclosure that Jesus is the Lord of history guarantees that they will receive the inheritance provided for them.

A Concealed Message

Many readers have felt that Revelation is a "closed" book. Its pictorial images and symbolism, the shifting perspective which is normal to the world of dreams and visions, and its strange expression have encouraged the opinion that the last book in the New Testament is also the most difficult to understand. This situation is unfortunate because the book presents itself as an unveiling of the truth (1:1); and a special blessing is pronounced upon the one who reads the book (1:3). The final instruction in Revelation is the command: "Do not seal up the words of the prophecy of this book" (22:10). The book was prepared to comfort and to challenge the Christians of Asia to remain steadfast in their commitment to the Lord in spite of imperial persecution. It is clear that they must have understood the message of the book.

Part of the strangeness of the book may have been deliberate. John was writing under difficult circumstances, and it may have been necessary to convey the truth under a "coded" form in order to get his manuscript past the Roman guards on Patmos. A reader with little knowledge of the Old Testament and of the truth of the gospel will find in Revelation only strange and bizarre visions, the disturbed dreams of a madman. But the message would not remain concealed from the church leaders to whom it was addressed and the congregations for whom it was prepared.

There is another reason, however, why Revelation seems difficult to modern readers. Although the book is prophecy, it has been given an *apocalyptic* form, and the majority of Christians today have no understanding of this form which was familiar to both Jews and Christians in John's day. The essential element in apocalyptic is its view of history: history is seen as the stage on which the dramatic struggle between good and evil and between God and Satan is acted out. That means that the course of events in the present, visible world is determined by what has taken place in the invisible heavenly world. This perspective is the key to chapter 12, for example, which describes the vision of the woman and the dragon. The action of the dragon in seeking to destroy the woman's son (12:4,5) and in waging war with the rest of her children (12:17) clearly describes the demonic character of the persecution of the church. The disruptive action against the church is the result of Satan's defeat in the heavenly realm (12:7-9). Unable to sustain himself where God is the sovereign Lord, Satan turns his fury against the people of God in the world.

The agent of God in history is the church, while the agent of Satan is the Roman Empire. The conflict of the empire with the church appears to involve men and women and conflicting theologies. But the apocalyptic mentality has the vision to see that it also involves God and Satan. The letter to the senior pastor of the church in Pergamum offers a vivid illustration of this angle of vision. The glorified Lord says: "I know where you live— where Satan has his throne. . . . You did not renounce your faith in me, even in the days of Antipas, my faithful witness, who was put to death in your city—where Satan lives" (2:13).

Satan's "throne" is a slightly veiled reference to the temple to the divine Augustus in the city. The occasion for Christian martyrdom was zeal for the Roman imperial cult. But in an apocalyptic perspective it makes little difference whether you speak about Rome or about Satan. The ultimate source of the conflict with the church is Satan, although he expresses his fury through the officials of the imperial cult. John says that Pergamum is the city where Satan lives.

Apocalyptic literature commonly uses symbolism to express its message, and this is true of Revelation as well. Many of the symbols have been drawn from the Old Testament Scriptures, but others require spiritual reflection. In chapter 13, for example, John sees a beast coming out of the sea who receives a throne and great authority from the dragon. Men worship the beast who is given power to make war against the saints and to conquer them (13:1-7). This beast is clearly a symbol for the Roman emperor, Domitian. John then sees another beast coming out of the earth who enforces the worship of the first beast (13:11-17). This second beast is a symbol for the officials of the imperial cult.

In the later visions John sees two cities, and two women. The city of Babylon (16:19; 17:5—18:24) is a coded representation of the Roman Empire where the people of God are once more in captivity. A prostitute, dressed in scarlet and glittering with jewels, is the symbol of Rome (17:18). The other city is Jerusalem, the Holy City and the dwelling place of God (21:1-27). A pure woman, "prepared as a bride beautifully dressed for her husband" (21:2), is the symbol of Jerusalem, or the church. The contrast is deliberate and helped the Christians of Asia to see the conflict between Rome and the church in visual terms. The message of Revelation was never intended to be concealed from God's people. The book declares the triumph of God in history through the death and resurrection of Jesus Christ who now reigns as Lord of the church and the Lord of history, and it calls all Christians to remain faithful to the Lord (13:10).

NOTES

1. Tacitus *Annals of Rome* 15.44.
2. Ovid *Metamorphoses* 8.626ff.
3. Abrosiastor *Works* 3.373.
4. Suetonius *Life of the Deified Claudius* 24.4.
5. *Sententia Pauli* 5.21.1.
6. Tacitus *Annals of Rome* 13.11.2, 27.6, 43.7; 14.45.4; Suetonius *Life of Nero* 10.2.
7. Eusebius *Church History* 2.22.
8. Tacitus *Annals of Rome* 15.44.
9. Suetonius *Life of the Deified Claudius* 25.4.
10. Suetonius *Life of Domitian* 13.